PRAISE FOR

THE
HABITS
OF HIGHLY
EFFECTIVE
CHURCHES

The nine habits of highly effective churches serve as a benchmark list against which churches can measure their effectiveness in the service of the Lord. Borrowing this book is sufficient only if you have everything George Barna has written, you go to one of his conferences at least every two years, and you just want to take a quick look at his new material. But I warn you, you will buy your own copy after you take a peek.

GEORGE BULLARD
Executive Director and Head Coach, New Reformation Solutions
Columbia, South Carolina

George Barna here demonstrates a comprehensive understanding of the vital elements of healthy church growth. His style is straightforward, his information is well-supported by ongoing research, and his approach is practical. This is a valuable resource for pastors of churches large and small, old and new, denominational and independent.

DR. EDDIE GIBBS
Donald A. McGavran Professor of Church Growth
Fuller Theological Seminary, Pasadena, California

Who among us understands the American church at large better than George Barna? *Habits of Highly Effective Churches* is another shining example of Barna's keen analysis, sharp insight and God-given passion for preparing the Bride of Christ for His return.

TED HAGGARD
Senior Pastor, New Life Church
Colorado Springs, Colorado

Whether you like Barna or not, you can't afford to not read him. (Incidentally, I like him.)

JACK W. HAYFORD
Pastor, The Church On The Way
President, The King's Seminary
Van Nuys, California

If you care about holistic spiritual formation and the health of the local church, then George Barna's book is for you. Master these habits and transformation is sure to follow!

STEPHEN A. MACCHIA
President, Vision New England
Author of *Becoming a Healthy Church*
Acton, Massachusetts

Like few other people I know, George Barna has his finger on the pulse of the American church. *Habits of Highly Effective Churches* lays out proven strategies for any church that wants to be a vibrant place of dynamic worship and ministry. I'm excited about the impact this book could have on our churches. I *highly* recommend it!

BILL MCCARTNEY
Founder and President, Promise Keepers
Denver, Colorado

The Habits of Highly Effective Churches is the silver bullet that kills common Christian misconceptions about what makes up a "successful" congregation. George Barna's rigorous pursuit for truth and thorough research reveal haunting lessons for every local church in America today. In the Lord's economy, it is not the size of our budget, vast numbers of people attending or a host of programs that make a winning congregation; rather a successful church is built on repeated behaviors in line with God's wisdom—healthy habits!

JOHN C. MAXWELL
Author, Speaker and Founder of The INJOY Group
Atlanta, Georgia

Let me caution you who are considering reading this book: Get prepared to have your comfortable ideas and church practices challenged. George Barna offers incredible insights which can't help but motivate you to strive toward making your church more effective.

RANDY POPE
Pastor, Perimeter Church
Duluth, Georgia

Few individuals have gained more insight about the true nature of today's churches than George Barna. This book is not another survey of what all churches do, but rather it is focused on the most essential differences between the great churches and the good ones. *Habits of Highly Effective Churches* is a blockbuster! You will not want to miss it!

C. PETER WAGNER
Chancellor, Wagner Leadership Institute
Colorado Springs, Colorado

Being Strategic in Your God-Given Ministry

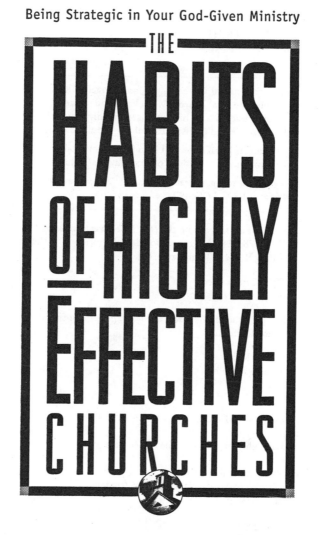

THE HABITS OF HIGHLY EFFECTIVE CHURCHES

GEORGE BARNA

Regal

A Division of Gospel Light
Ventura, California, U.S.A.

PUBLISHED BY REGAL BOOKS
A DIVISION OF GOSPEL LIGHT
VENTURA, CALIFORNIA, U.S.A.
PRINTED IN U.S.A.

Regal Books is a ministry of Gospel Light, an evangelical Christian publisher dedicated to serving the local church. We believe God's vision for Gospel Light is to provide church leaders with biblical, user-friendly materials that will help them evangelize, disciple and minister to children, youth and families.

It is our prayer that this Regal book will help you discover biblical truth for your own life and help you meet the needs of others. May God richly bless you.

For a free catalog of resources from Regal Books/Gospel Light please contact your Christian supplier or contact us at 1-800-4-GOSPEL.

This book was first published as *The Habits of Highly Effective Churches* in 1998 by Issachar Resources in Ventura, California.

Cover Design by Kevin Keller
Interior Design by Rob Williams
Edited by Wil Simon

LIBRARY OF CONGRESS CATALOGING-IN-PUBLICATION DATA
Barna, George.
    The habits of highly effective churches / George Barna.
        p. cm.
    Includes bibliographical references.
    ISBN 0830718559 (hc) — ISBN 0830718605 (trade)
    1. Christian leadership. I. Title.

BV652.1 .B362 2000   99-049020
253—dc21

1 2 3 4 5 6 7 8 9 10 11 12 13 14 15 / 09 08 07 06 05 04 03 02 01 00

Rights for publishing this book in other languages are contracted by Gospel Literature International (GLINT). GLINT also provides technical help for the adaptation, translation and publishing of Bible study resources and books in scores of languages worldwide. For further information, contact GLINT, P.O. Box 4060, Ontario, CA 91761-1003, U.S.A. You may also send E-mail to Glintint@aol.com or visit their website at www.glint.org.

CONTENTS

ACKNOWLEDGMENTS————————

This book is the outgrowth of a seminar (Inward, Outward & Upward: Ministry That Transforms Lives) and various research projects conducted by the Barna Research Group, Ltd. (BRG) from 1997 to 1999. We at BRG operate as a team. It is my privilege, therefore, to acknowledge the help I have received from my colleagues at BRG that has led to the development of this book. In alphabetical order let me note my particular gratitude to the efforts of Rachel Ables, Pam Jacob, David Kinnaman, Jill Kinnaman, Sarah Polley, Celeste Rivera and Margaret Wells. Each of these professionals has been instrumental in my ability to deliver information and analysis to church leaders for the benefit of churches and the greater glory of God. I am thankful that God has brought together this team of people who share a common vision of serving Him by helping His Church.

I am also grateful to my wife and coworker, Nancy Barna, for the various roles she has played in this process. For nearly two decades she has been a supportive partner in the work of Barna Research. Now that she is devoting most of her energy to being a mother to our two children, her input into projects such as this one has required an even greater sacrifice on her part. Her willingness to assist in whatever ways are necessary for the good of our ministry has been a compelling lesson to me.

I must also thank the many churches, pastors and Christians across the nation who shared their time, experience and insights with me and with our company as we conducted this research. Without their help, this project would never have been born. Their assistance is yet another reflection of the Church at work, showing a greater spirit of cooperation than competition and a deeper concern for transformation than for public credit. May God repay them each a thousandfold for the blessing they have been to us and to many others through this book.

INTRODUCTION—LETTERS FROM THE FRONT

I receive numerous letters from church leaders all over the country concerning the challenges churches face these days. Sometimes the letters are written to share good news about ministry victories; other letters describe the heartbreak and hardships resulting from well-intended but ineffective ministry. There is little doubt in my mind that the Church in America lives in an age that is pregnant with opportunity. But exploiting that opportunity is neither easy nor costless.

Here are a couple of relevant examples of the difficult choices and conditions that church leaders must address every day. Can you relate to these situations?

Dear Mr. Barna:
I am the pastor of a church that was started 86 years ago. At one time, it was the largest church in the area, attracting more than 1000 worshipers each weekend. The church was known locally for the warmth of its people and the excellence of its ministry programs. The preaching has always been strong biblically.

Having read your latest book, I figure you are one person who can understand the dilemma I find myself in today. I was hired as the pastor of this declining congregation seven years ago. Attendance is down to around 200 people, and slowly dropping. The "gray-hairs" dominate the pews on Sunday mornings. Our limited efforts to reach younger people have borne little fruit. We have tried to update our ministry—the music, the pew Bibles, the signage, our logo, the appearance of our buildings and so forth. While our long time members are proud of these improvements, very few others would even be aware of the upgrades.

I am indebted to you and a few others who study churches and inform us of where we may have departed from the path or what some other churches have discovered that has helped them to make inroads in their communities. But to be quite honest, I'm awfully confused. I'm not blaming you for that, I'm just hoping that perhaps you can give me some specific guidance as to what I should do at this point. I'm willing to give this church all the energy I have left—I'm 46 at the moment; this is my fourth pastorate—but I don't want to squander what energy I have.

In a nutshell here's my dilemma. I've been to seminary, which taught me how to exegete the Scriptures in their original languages and how to teach people the substance of God's Word. I've attended seminars that have focused on all kinds of additional duties—organizational skills, worship, fund-raising, counseling, leadership, service ministries, etc. I report to a board of elders, 12 men who have at least 12 different ideas of where the church should be going and just as many suggested routes to get us there. And I've made the obligatory pilgrimages to the big churches, only to return frustrated that I don't have 10,000-plus people flocking to my facilities every week.

Simply put, I don't understand how to weave all the knowledge and experiences I've collected over the years into a coherent package of activities, or maybe a philosophy of church, that would propel me in a viable direction. I can see how bits and pieces of what I've learned might be helpful. But I don't understand how to put it all together.

Have you written something addressing this problem, or do you know of some resource that speaks to this issue? I'm open to new ideas; I'm even open to starting over, from scratch, to make sense of all of this. I look forward to hearing from you.

Yours in Christ,
JOHN ROWLAND, PASTOR

Dear Mr. Barna:

Your seminar was very stimulating. The lay leaders who accompanied me felt overwhelmed after the opening session, but were quite excited by the end of the day as they considered the great opportunities that lie before us. Thank you for clarifying the issues and giving us common ground to work from as we labor together to honor our Lord.

Would you answer a nagging question for me? During the seminar you described aspects of how certain churches have overcome cultural resistance and made their faith relevant without compromising their beliefs and values. But how do those particular efforts fit into the larger framework of ministry activity?

As the pastor of this church I have to take responsibility for all of the ministry ventures of our congregation. I cannot, of course, focus on one or two dimensions to the exclusion of all else we do. Your seminar did not suggest that course of action, but can you give me some ideas regarding how other churches have put the principles and applications you described into a more comprehensive framework of a church? Any information along those lines would be greatly appreciated, especially now that our leaders are anxious to make some changes and see new ideas and programs implemented.

Thank you for your work and for your love for the Church.

Until He returns,
HENRY PETERSON

Have you ever felt as if you were stuck between having great information and opportunities but not having enough of the big picture to make bold ministry moves? Or perhaps you are the type of person who is willing to take chances in ministry, but only after having thought through a long-term plan of action in which all of today's moves impact (and are impacted by) all of next month's efforts.

The issue at hand is how to be effective in ministry. And being effective cannot be addressed unless we approach matters strategically. That is what we will discuss in this book: how you can influence your ministry to be highly effective. Significant impact demands a strategic approach to ministry. The objective of this book is to describe how several thousand churches around the nation have learned to think and act strategically, holding fast to their theological beliefs and related values, so that they could become effective agents of Christian ministry.

To some extent this is a book about church growth, but it is about corporate and personal spiritual growth rather than increased attendance. This is also a book about church health—taken from the perspective of spiritual depth. But more than anything, this is a book about how to have a holistic, church-based ministry in which people's lives are revolutionized through the assistance of their church. The prescriptions offered are based upon the practical experience of numerous churches across America. Those churches come from a wide variety of denominations, from all geographic regions, across all ethnic and racial lines and include churches of different sizes and ages.

This is a book for anyone who wants his/her church to be effective in ministry.

What Is "Effective" Ministry?

Before we get into the prescriptions we must understand some of the basic terms. The cornerstone term is "effective." Throughout this book, I will describe a ministry as being effective when lives are transformed such that people are constantly enabled to become more Christ-like. Effective ministries foster significant and continual changes in how people live. When your church is able to consistently facilitate a personal metamorphosis among its people, then it is operating in the realm of effectiveness.

In our culture it is easy to get confused about what "effective ministry" looks like at the grassroots level. Our interviews with pastors and laity confirm that there is a tremendous degree of confusion about the practical meaning of effective ministry. For instance, we know that many Christians believe that each of the following is an indisputable mark of an effective church:

- having a sanctuary filled with 1,000 (or more) people at the weekend service;
- raising a million dollars a year (or more) for the church's ministry;
- donating a half-million dollars or more annually to global missions;
- adding buildings or constructing a new campus with at least 100,000 square feet of ministry facilities;
- sending church choirs to sing in churches, community events and on school campuses throughout the nation or overseas;
- broadcasting the church worship services throughout the city, region or country;
- offering a wide range of Christian education classes and ministry programs;
- having high name awareness in the community at large;
- adding 100 (or more) new members in a year.

Contrary to popular opinion, these scenarios do not necessarily reflect a church that is truly effective. If effective relates to personal commitments and activities through which people become more Christlike, the situations just described do not automatically signal either corporate or personal spiritual health.

Attendance figures, square footage, staff size, annual operating budget and the like are simplistic, sometimes misleading measures that overlook the most important aspect of any ministry—the hearts of the people. There are many churches that offer a smorgasbord of ministry events and meetings but in which the participants are simply going through the motions. In fact, most churches that go through a horrendous collapse but eventually regain ministry effectiveness facilitate a turnaround by *reducing* the number of programs, services, events and other activities available.

I'm willing to bet that when the Lord examines a church His criteria have little to do with attendance statistics, budgeting complexities or program breadth. If His critique of the Pharisees and other religious leaders is any indication, His analysis will hinge on the depth of people's commitment to making their faith real and pure. Tiny congregations composed of people completely dedicated to being a blessing to God and others will probably make the grade; churches that have a high profile and earn constant media attention but exhibit limited spiritual growth and depth may be surprised (as in heartbroken) at how they fare in His judgment scheme.

SIX PILLARS OF EFFECTIVENESS

Some churches have discovered how to become effective in one or two dimensions of ministry. I frequently encounter churches that are effective in an area such as Christian education or creating an intrachurch community. Many churches become known for one particular aspect of ministry such as Christian education or community service, but generally struggle in other core ministry areas. It is very unusual to find a church that has developed a truly holistic ministry—effective in the six dimensions of ministry that constitute a complete church.

What are those six dimensions? They are the very aspects that characterized the Early Church: worship, evangelism, Christian education, community among the believers, stewardship and serving the needy. These might be considered the six pillars of church ministry. When a church is doing superb work in each of these elements of ministry, it is truly being the Church that Christ intended us to be.

Throughout this book, when I refer to being "highly effective," I am alluding to churches that are doing a great job in regard to these six pillars. In other words, these are churches where the people are implementing Christianity more and more *deeply*, both on the corporate and individual levels. They are people who truly worship God on a regular basis. They are people who are consistently introducing non-Christians to Christ. They are learning and applying principles and truths of the Christian faith to their lives. They are developing significant relationships with other believers, befriending, encouraging and holding each other accountable. They joyfully contribute their material possessions to ministries and individuals in need, for the glory of God. And they devote their time and energy to helping disadvantaged people. Cumulatively, these behaviors represent the Church in its fullest manifestation.

THE SCOPE OF THE PROBLEM

If being highly effective is defined in this way then the American Church has a serious problem. Bluntly stated, my research suggests that only 10 to 15 percent of the Protestant churches in our nation today can be deemed highly effective.

The good news is that when that figure is projected nationally it corresponds to 30,000 to 50,000 churches that qualify as highly effective ministries. That's a lot of churches, no matter how you slice it! But the other side of the coin must be considered, too: There are more than a quarter of a million churches in America that are not highly effective in ministry—roughly nine out of every 10 churches! If you believe, as I do, that the Church is the single most important organization in America, then this situation is of crisis proportions.

Fortunately, you will discover what my study of effective churches has found time after time: Any church that is truly desirous of being highly effective can become such a ministry. Creating (or sustaining) a highly effective church is not rocket science. God has not called a select handful to be highly effective while the rest of us watch in awe and experience personal despair over our own limitations and inabilities in ministry. Thousands and thousands of churches are doing highly effective work for Christ today and your church can become one of those bodies, if it hasn't already. All it takes is a commitment to follow some basic guidelines, good leadership, the determination to be and remain highly effective and, of course, God's blessing.

The Role of Habits

One of the ministry secrets among highly effective churches is reliance upon good habits. Once again, a definition is in order. A habit is a repeated behavior. Highly effective churches have a transforming impact on people's lives because they have developed habits that facilitate specified ministry outcomes—outcomes that are consistent with Scripture and that emphasize life transformation.

My research has clearly shown that every church has dozens of habits, but not all repeated behaviors are of equal value. Some habits are detrimental. This is readily apparent outside of ministry. For instance, we speak of someone having a drug habit (i.e., the repeated use of harmful drugs) and know that such a habit is potentially lethal. Other habits can be pernicious, too—smoking, overeating, talking too much, spending all of one's money, swearing, cheating, lying, stealing, never returning telephone calls, etc.

Take a few minutes to identify some of the many habits that define your church's ministry. In working with churches I have seen how most churches have little, if any, conscious awareness of their ministry's habits. For example, most churches that possess the following habits that are detrimental to their ministry are unaware of those habits and their effects. Consequently they have no intention of addressing those harmful, repeated behaviors.

Harmful Habits

- *Printing the Bible verses used in a sermon, in the service bulletin or projecting them on a large screen*
  This has encouraged many people to stop carrying their Bibles to church and ultimately from using them through the week.

- *Conducting an annual Easter and/or Christmas event*
  These events begin with great intentions but fizzle after a few years. These activities attract few of the outsiders they were originally intended to attract.

- *Maintaining a rigid order of service in the weekend event*
  There is value to stability and consistency, but the predictability of the service has created disenchantment among many, especially Baby Busters, both because it is too routine and because the message communicated is one of resistance to change in a world defined by change.

- *Expecting the pastor's spouse to be the catchall*
  Thousands of churches continue to pay one (below average) salary, ostensibly for the pastor, but expect output from two full-time employees (the pastor and his/her spouse). This not only creates emotional and financial

stress for the pastor's family but facilitates unrealistic productivity expectations by the congregation.

- *Requiring the pastor to be the chief fund-raiser for the church*
This undermines the trust people have in their pastor. The congregation never knows why the pastor is saying or doing something: Is it because it needs to be said or because it will facilitate generous giving?

- *Developing an information-laden website*
Currently more than 98 percent of the church websites we have examined are designed to provide static information to people. The individuals most likely to use a church site and to find it useful, however, are those under 30, and they are looking for interactive possibilities, not information.

- *Assuming that community is fostered in a handshake*
Setting aside a minute in the weekend service to allow people to shake the hands of those seated nearby is not by itself a bad thing. It is when the church's leaders assume, however, that the exercise has anything to do with building community, establishing interpersonal intimacy or creating a friendly atmosphere that the practice becomes an unhealthy habit.

- *Maintaining church classes or programs because of internal politics or history*
Often congregations do not have sufficient interest in a class or program to support its retention or perhaps

> there is not sufficient expertise available to conduct the
> activity with excellence. In response to various types of
> pressure, though, most churches have one or more pro-
> grams that continue in spite of ample evidence that the
> program is innocuous at best and harmful at worst.

In effect, these habits are harmful because they have become
counterproductive. Every one of them was initiated with good
intent. Most of them probably had a positive effect for a period
of time. Eventually, however, each of these habits became the
antithesis of its original purpose. As a habit, though, it is either
beyond our framework of analysis or has become such an
ingrained behavior that we are no longer cognizant of its existence—it just happens because it has always happened.

To avoid creating bad habits in ministry—and frankly, most
churches have a number of unfortunate habits—we must be very
conscious of what we do, when we do it, why we do it and the
outcome of those actions. As we evaluate our ministry behaviors,
we should incorporate the positive behaviors into our habit-pat-
tern. In seeking to distinguish the positive from the negative
ministry habits, realize that there are four elements that make a
habit desirable:

- *Intentional Behavior*
  The challenge is to think specifically about what we
  are doing. Aristotle once said that the unexamined life
  is not worth living. Similarly, the unintentional ministry activity is not worth doing unless we can justify
  its implementation. A ministry effort that is unintentional is not one that we can rely upon to help people

become more Christlike or to enable a church to become highly effective.

- ### *Strategic Behavior*
  A habit becomes strategic when it is done purposefully and in relation to a specified desirable outcome. Habits that are not strategic have no place in ministry, they simply consume precious resources for no valid end. To maximize the strategic character of a behavior, the behavior should be consistent with the mission, vision and values of the church.

- ### *Productive Behavior*
  While ministry is not a business, per se, effective ministry requires that we use our limited resources to produce an important product: changed lives. If a habit is not useful in moving us closer to that goal, it is not productive. If it is not productive, it is counterproductive and therefore detrimental. You should be able to identify how a given habit produces benefit to your ministry.

- ### *Biblical Behavior*
  It is possible to be intentional, strategic and productive but to be outside the boundaries provided by Scripture. Every habit must be examined in light of God's principles and parameters. This is especially imperative for ministries since many individuals take their life cues from the habits of churches.

Highly effective churches have numerous habits, but they are habits that are intentional, strategic, productive and biblically consistent. That is what enables them to be highly effective ministries.

The Nine Habits That Matter

My recent research has discovered that there are nine habits possessed by all highly effective churches. Those habits are put into practice in different ways, but the essence of those habits is the same across all highly effective churches. Here are those nine highly effective church habits in a nutshell:

Beneficial Habits

Habit #1
Rely upon strategic leadership.

Habit #2
Organize to facilitate highly effective ministry.

Habit #3
Emphasize developing significant relationships within the congregation.

Habit #4
Congregants invest themselves in genuine worship.

Habit #5
Engage in strategic evangelism.

Habit #6
Get people involved in systematic theological growth.

Habit #7
Utilize holistic stewardship practices.

Habit #8
Serve the needy people in the community.

Habit #9
Equip families to minister to themselves.

Each of these habits requires an approach to ministry that is different from the norm. But it is the combination of these nine habits—and the many activities that make up each of those habits—that enables a church to transcend survival to become highly effective. We will address each of these habits in a subsequent chapter.

COMMITMENT TO BE EFFECTIVE

If God has called your church into existence, then He intends to bless it. If you are serious about becoming and staying highly effective, let me provide one way of understanding what makes a church an agency of significant life transformation: While you cannot imitate everything that a highly effective church does and expect to be similarly life changing, *understanding these nine principles of ministry and adapting them to the unique vision and resource base God has given you will enable your church to become highly effective, too.*

The major factor left to your discretion will be the commitment to deploy godly, gifted leaders to facilitate such ministry and an unflagging commitment to strive to become all that God intends for your church to become. Are you willing to make such a commitment?

ENSURING THAT LEADERS DIRECT THE CHURCH

 My family and friends know that one of my weaknesses is watching professional basketball games. During the playoffs each spring my jam-packed schedule suddenly contains multiple free evenings, enabling me to watch the key games leading up to the finals. The finals themselves are a near-religious experience for me. It's a safe bet that I will be stretched out, pretzels and Coke by my side, transfixed six feet from the family TV set for every game of the finals.

Not much comes between those games and me. Several years ago I was on a ministry trip in Asia during the finals. My partners on the trip marveled at my ability to cajole the bartender in one of the lounges in the Jakarta, Indonesia, airport to tune the satellite TV to game four of the series. (I was probably the only person in the lounge area who even understood the language of the broadcast.)

Given this passion for hoops, it shouldn't surprise you that for years I have respected Michael Jordan—"His Airness"—as a phenomenal ballplayer. Although my nature is to reject products, services or people that are overhyped, no basketball aficionado would even contemplate denying Jordan's incredible ability. He is the consummate "money player"—the kind who can be counted on to do whatever needs to be done to win a game: score, pass, defend, rebound, set screens, direct the offense. In the deciding moments of a game, Michael is "The Man."

But the 1998 NBA Finals enabled me to experience a different side of Michael Jordan. I expected him to score big and to play killer defense, but what the network cameras revealed during the Bulls' rematch with the Utah Jazz was something even more impressive: *Michael's leadership abilities*. This entailed more than taking the pressure shots, barking out plays or telling a teammate where to position himself for optimal offensive impact. Watching the six-game series against Utah, I noticed the following:

- Michael passionately chewing out several teammates for their failure to show sufficient intensity or for mental lapses that resulted in busted plays;
- Michael jawing with the referees more than usual, exploiting his superstar status to challenge the refs' judgment and hopefully enhance the prospects of gaining favorable calls for his team later in the contest;

- Michael identifying gaps in the opponents' defense to his coach, Phil Jackson, and suggesting strategies that could break down the Jazz' defense;
- Michael, the highest-paid yet hardest working man on the floor, purposefully seating himself during a time out next to a teammate who was not playing so that he could instruct that reserve about an important detail of the game that would eventually help the reserve to maximize his limited time on the floor during that crucial game;
- Michael, the heart and soul of the team, was clearly ticked off with himself after he made a couple of bonehead plays that the Jazz took advantage of to build into a larger lead. But rather than verbally apologize to his teammates and back off for a few minutes to personally regroup, Michael simply stepped up the pace. He apologized by blocking a shot on the first offensive set, causing an errant pass on the next trip down the floor, then scoring on a difficult, twisting jump shot the next time he touched the ball;
- Michael completely dominating both ends of the floor in the last minute of the final game to single-handedly bring his team back from a deficit to win their sixth championship of the decade.

What struck me, in other words, was not that a great athlete was playing a remarkable game under incredible pressure. What floored me was how great a leader Michael Jordan was. In his 44 minutes on the court in that final game he was the essence of leadership. Through his intelligence, heart and physical skill he motivated his teammates to play at a higher level. He orchestrated the activities of his colleagues to maximize their respective talents and abilities. He respectfully took direction from his coach, Phil Jackson, and converted Jackson's ideas into real-time, creative solutions in the midst of the mayhem on the court. Jordan demonstrated courage by standing up to the taller, stronger, menacing power forwards of the Jazz, just as he reflected it through his strategic verbal jousting with the referees. And above all, he embodied an indomitable spirit, an unquenchable desire to win. He was, as one of the network announcers said, "a man on a mission."

The Bulls may or may not have won that day without his 45 points, four steals and tough defense. But I guarantee you they would not have won without his leadership.

Michael Jordans in the Pastorate

Having studied thousands of churches across America, I am similarly struck by one of the requisite habits of highly effective churches: they are led by strong leaders. Churches that are serious agencies of life transformation have leaders who possess the same qualities as Michael Jordan:

- a vision of what they seek to create;
- a respect-based relationship with a team of competent colleagues;
- effective communication skills;
- a strategic mind and purposeful courage;
- an unquenchable passion about the outcome to which they are committed.

Almost every church has someone in a position of leadership, typically with the title of Pastor. But the highly effective churches have learned to distinguish between having someone in a position of leadership and having a leader in charge. The unfortunate truth is that most American churches have pastors who are not leaders. And my surveys show that most of the true leaders in our churches are not pastors. Let's explore this further.

To be an effective leader, one must be called by God to lead, possess the character of a person of God, and demonstrate a group of competencies that result in leadership. A leader implements the gift and ability to lead by motivating, mobilizing, resourcing and directing people to pursue a jointly shared vision from God.[1]

In other words, to be an effective leader you need not win the preaching award, nor must you be a great manager of the ministry, or a wise counselor of parishioners who have emotional problems. Such abilities are often counterproductive for a true leader. A great leader is more likely to *delegate* preaching, administration, counseling, fundraising, evangelism and program development. Doing so frees him/her to focus on the heart of leadership necessities: communicating and gaining widespread ownership of the vision, strategic thinking, creative problem solving, team building, conflict resolution, long-term planning, development of future leaders, evaluation of the ministry and opportunities, etc.

Given this perspective, it should be clear that having a title or position of pastor does not make you a leader any more than swimming in the ocean makes you a fish. Our interviews with nationwide, representative samples of Protestant pastors consistently show that most pastors do not even consider themselves to be leaders. Fewer than one out of every 20 pastors believes he/she has the spiritual gift of leadership. Fewer than one out of every four pastors claims to serve the church as a true leader. Most of them feel they have been called, trained and hired to preach and teach. Leadership, for most pastors, is just one of those unfortunate duties they must endure as part of the deal that allows them to do that which really turns them on—preaching and teaching.

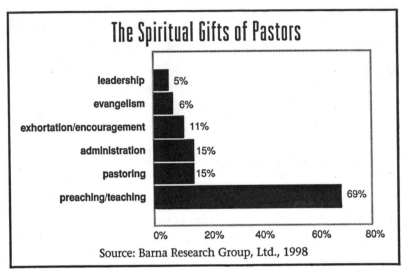

The Spiritual Gifts of Pastors

Gift	Percentage
leadership	5%
evangelism	6%
exhortation/encouragement	11%
administration	15%
pastoring	15%
preaching/teaching	69%

Source: Barna Research Group, Ltd., 1998

Figure 1.1

Highly effective churches, on the other hand, have placed a true leader in the position of leadership. In all honesty, this often happens by mistake rather than by design, but the end result is the same: when a true leader is given the opportunity to lead a church, people's lives are never the same. The entire culture of the church changes because of its pastor's leadership. Such leaders articulate vision, mobilize the people, motivate focused activity, consistently provide strategic direction and resources to get the job done efficiently and effectively—these churches alter history, *one life at a time.*

In recent years I have observed that most churches confuse superb preaching with effective leadership. The ability to differentiate between these two elements is perhaps the simplest way of distinguishing effective churches from educational churches.

There is nothing wrong with having a church that provides great preaching—every church benefits from dynamic, biblical, application-oriented preaching! However, most of the great preachers in America are not great leaders—nor do they aspire to be. Outstanding preachers feel called to preach God's Word to the best of their ability and, to their credit, they devote many of their waking hours to studying the Scriptures, developing ways of conveying important information in comprehensible ways and finding the perfect illustrations to drive home crucial points.

But living for the purpose of preaching solid biblical sermons is a world apart from casting vision, building a world-class ministry team, planning for the future, and doing the myriad of other activities that consume the mind and energy of a true leader. As I have written more extensively elsewhere, preaching and leading represent different gifts, callings and activities. Neither is more important than the other; they're just different.[2] But expecting one person to provide both is placing an unreasonable expectation upon the pastor.

Finding An Effective Leader

I have been surprised to discover that more often than not, churches hire leaders by mistake. Typically, the church is looking for a pastor who preaches, performs the sacraments and can supervise the administrative tasks of the church. Sometimes, in the process of examining candidates, the church is attracted to a particular individual who possesses something unique—a quality of personal character, a certainty of pastoral calling and evidence of the ability to make good things happen. That candidate is often hired without the church understanding the real person with whom it has entered into a covenant. It is not until much later that some within the congregation recognize the magnificent blessing God has bestowed upon them by bringing a true leader to the church.

There seem to be four ways in which a church attracts and installs a true leader as its pastor:

- ### *A History of Hiring Great Leaders*

  Some highly effective churches have a great leader because at some point in the history of the church a true leader assumed the pastorate. Sometimes this happens from day one, when an entrepreneurial leader, using his or her gifts for God's work, plants a new church and soon creates a viable community of faith out of vision, prayer, intentional relationships and months and months of hard work. Sometimes the church is not so fortunate; it goes through a succession of ineffective pastors before it stumbles upon a great leader and slowly wakes up to the treasure it has received from God. Whatever the historical trail may have been, *these congregations become addicted to great leadership.*

  When the initial leader/pastor gets ready to pass the baton to a successor, that leader and the people know they need someone of the same nature and caliber to continue the job. Consequently, such churches have an enviable history of attracting and following great leaders.

- ### *Pastoral Search Team Intentionally Identifies and Successfully Hires a True Leader*

  More often than not this happens because the members of the search team are leaders themselves or are lay people savvy enough to recognize the difference between those who can lead and those who just think they can lead. Having suffered through one or more pastorates of well-intentioned pastors who could not lead, the search team purposefully seeks a gifted leader to turn around the ministry fortunes of the church.

- ### *Strong Credentials and Teaching Ability of the Pastoral Candidate*
These churches typically are impressed by the preaching of a pastoral candidate and decide that the candidate's preaching skills are so strong as to justify a call to the pastorate. Much to their surprise, the congregation soon discovers that it got more than it bargained for—in fact, it got something it did not even realize it was lacking and sorely needed: leadership. The attractive qualities of the candidate were merely well-honed secondary abilities that are part of the skill mix for effective leadership. Eventually, the insightful members of the congregation recognize that a great leader is always an effective communicator. Preaching is often a noteworthy skill of great leaders, but is simply one of many critical tools in his/her leadership toolbox.

- ### *The Church Desperate for a New Pastor*
These are usually churches in pain—undergoing tragedies like severe membership loss, an absence of vision and passion for ministry, a congregational split, staggering financial debt, etc. When a leader applies for such a job, the church is struck by something unusual that the individual brings to the table: realistic hope for

the church's future. Smitten by the possibility that the future could be glorious after all, they lock onto a true leader with a forceful vision. The contagious passion of this leader calls the Body to a greater future that shatters the chains of despair, self-pity and hopelessness.

It is important to know that there is a more recent and increasingly common phenomenon occurring among churches that are headed by a true leader. These are churches where the senior pastor recognizes that he/she is not a leader, understands how much the congregation needs a leader at the helm and then honestly confronts the congregation with these insights. With the permission and blessing of the congregation, that senior pastor then joins forces with someone who is truly a leader. The result is that the senior pastor may step aside and allow the true leader to have the position of senior pastor. Alternatively, the original pastor may keep the title but relinquish the leadership responsibilities and authority to the true leader. Where such transitions occur the courageous steps taken by the original pastor certainly confirm his/her own calling to ministry, submission to the will of God and complete love for the church through such an act of self-knowledge and humility.

What happens to the original pastor who was honest and bold enough to admit that he/she was not a leader? Often, that person will remain on staff at the church, using the gift that God has given to him/her, usually that of preaching or teaching, for the benefit of the congregation. In fact, the leader who emerges is often a lay person who agrees to use the gift that God has given to him/her to help the church progress while developing a strong team of ministry peers to facilitate the ministry opportunities facing the church. One of the key players on that team is the former pastor, whose gift for teaching and preaching frees the newly appointed leader to do what he/she does best—lead.

More and more churches are pursuing this path. Perhaps this is not surprising since it is a biblical model. If you study the leaders described in the Bible you soon discover that every great leader called by God worked with a strong team of ministry associates. The fact that churches are now embracing a leader-led, multiple-person, team-based ministry is exciting and certainly bodes well for the future of the American Church.

Positioning the Leader to Succeed

Highly effective churches set up their leader/pastor for success. The ways in which this happens vary from church to church, but here are some of the most common ways in which this is done:

*The responsibilities of the leader/pastor are
focused and limited.*

Many churches make a grievous mistake: They expect their pastor to be the master of all trades. The expectations set for most pastors doom them to failure before they begin their work. These unrealistic expectations help to explain why pastoral burnout has grown to dangerous proportions. Our research has even shown that among a dozen types of professionals, pastors are the most frustrated of the lot, typically feeling guilt, stress and disappointment due to their inability to fulfill the demands placed upon them by their flocks. Our time management study among pastors indicated that the typical pastor juggles an extraordinary number of major tasks (16) during an average week. The result of this burden is that many pastors do a mediocre job in most of those tasks, to the chagrin of the pastor and congregation alike.

Highly effective churches have eliminated this recipe for failure by writing and adhering to a reasonable job description for the leader/pastor. They acknowledge that leading a church is a full-time job. Consequently, the ancillary tasks of preaching, administration, counseling and the like are delegated to other gifted staff or lay people. The leader/pastor is held responsible for leadership endeavors: articulating the vision, gaining ownership of the vision, identifying and developing teams, procuring the necessary resources, evaluating ministry quality, creating strategic plans, solving significant ministry problems, identifying or creating significant ministry opportunities, building cross-organizational relationships, resolving conflicts, communicating necessary information to the staff and congregation, etc. When contract renewal time rolls around, the discussion focuses on how well the leader/pastor has satisfied the leadership objectives that he/she agreed to pursue.

The leader/pastor is the primary change driver in the congregation.

Change is one of the most difficult realities for any group of people to embrace, but it is also one of the elements that most directly influences the personal and spiritual growth of the group. Leaders are integral to the health of a group because they are the chief change agents, motivating the group to view change positively and to invest themselves tirelessly in intentional and strategic changes.

The leaders/pastors of highly effective churches demonstrate this endless instigation of change. From service to service, event to event, meeting to meeting and sermon to sermon, they relentlessly introduce productive changes. Some of those changes are imperceptible, others are monumental—but a common denominator among all of these pastors is their commitment to creating a congregational culture that is addicted to fruitful change.

How do they create that culture? There seem to be five components in the process. First, they model change in their own life and ministry. This ranges from instituting overt changes (personal appearance, preaching style, members of their inner circle, leisure activities) to enacting more subtle transformations (frequency of preaching, involvement in church committees, evangelistic style). Good leaders know that they cannot expect people to do that which they will not do, therefore, modeling change is critical.

Second, they rely heavily on other ministry leaders who are adept at reading the environment and adapting to it (without compromising their beliefs). The leadership team requires a wide range of skills and abilities, only a handful of which the leader/pastor brings to the table. Every successful leader/pastor must be in touch with existing conditions and future potential. Leaning on the experience and insights of those who embrace the vision and can introduce fresh information and interpretations to the ministry serves as a supplement to the leader's intuitive inclinations.

Third, they insist that the church's dominant teachers integrate change-applications into their lessons. The leader/pastor may even instruct these teachers on ways of embroidering the value of change and effective means of changing into Sunday school lessons, small group discussions and committee agendas. Great leaders know that no matter how personally effective they are at communicating the reasons for and means to change, their sole voice isn't sufficient to cause the necessary changes to occur. Fortifying the message through the words of others both clarifies and reinforces the message and also reduces the potential for people to challenge its validity.

Fourth, leaders publicly support the efforts of individuals who demonstrate a serious commitment to significant change in their own lives and ministry. It is not unusual, for instance, for a church to have a new believer offer a "testimony" during a worship service concerning how they were saved. Highly effective churches use life testimonies that transcend the conversion experience. Whether that change involved a transformed behavior, a new set of relationships, a unique ideology that had dramatic consequences or an intensified commitment to a calling, the testimony is purposefully positioned to challenge other congregants to examine their commitment to personal development.

Finally, leaders provide strategic direction for the church that consistently pushes the church to grow by pushing the outer edges of its comfort zone. Several of the leader/pastors I interviewed alluded to the Revelation 3 passage about the church in Laodicea—the complacent, lukewarm church—as the antithetical model to what they were striving to achieve.

The leader/pastor is excluded from most of the decisions made in the church.

Don't misunderstand my point. I found that in highly effective churches the leader/pastor has the final say on all of the major decisions affecting the congregation. What was so unique about these churches, though, was that the leader/pastor was not even involved in the vast majority of decisions made in relation to the church. One of the immediate benefits of this condition is that the pastor was not a decision-making bottleneck in the church. The operations of the ministry could flow smoothly—and move quite rapidly—because the pastor did not have to place a personal stamp of approval on most of the decisions being made—even those involving money, facilities and personnel.

Again, this unusual approach to pastoral leadership was made possible by the discipline of restricting the leader/pastor's energy to those tasks that truly required personal attention and involvement. Thus, the pastor became the central figure in highly important matters that affected the entire church or its future, and became a symbolic leader in the hundreds of weekly decisions that did not require such expertise. This delineation of decisions into those of core and peripheral significance enabled the leader/pastor to be strategic.

Congregations that are not effective are often paralyzed by pastors who retain control over virtually every decision. Those pastors—who typically are not leaders—are often struggling with ego and self-image problems, resulting in their need to insist on making every judgment call. This behavior signals their failure to master one of the key arts of leadership; delegation.

Congregations that are not effective are often paralyzed by pastors who retain control over virtually every decision. This behavior signals their failure to master one of the key arts of leadership: delegation.

Delegation flows freely at highly effective churches because of four fundamental conditions. First, the leader/pastor knows that there is a hierarchy of importance regarding decisions and is secure in the ability to distinguish between those decisions that require personal input and those that do not.

Second, the leader/pastor realizes that he/she merely slows down the ministry by having a hand in everything. Aware that timing is an important factor in effective ministry, these leaders strive for a streamlined, efficient processes that makes the most of everyone's time. That knowledge, by itself, mandates that in a complex organization (such as a church) decisions must be made by more than one central entity.

Third, delegation fits these churches because they have a corps of qualified, well-trained and competent associate leaders in place. When the need for decisions arises, these associates are adept at making decisions in line with the church's vision, values and strategic plan. They have been so thoroughly indoctrinated with the vision, values, culture, goals and strategy of the church that requiring the involvement of the senior leader would amount to a vote of "no confidence" in the ability of the associates.

Finally, these churches typically work within a decision-making system in which bad decisions are detected through early-warning filters that have been carefully woven into the fabric of the process. Even if a bad decision is made and actions are triggered as a result, the process does not get far before the erroneous choice is apparent and can be redressed.

When it is time to evaluate the leader/pastor, the evaluation criteria relate to leadership factors, rather than to the usual quantitative factors.

The churches that have leaders are able to retain them only if they evaluate their leaders according to reasonable performance criteria. For leaders, that means getting away from the superficial factors that churches typically use to assess a pastor: personal popularity, adequacy of preaching, the church's numerical growth, meeting budget targets, theological accuracy and the absence of publicly known moral failures by the pastor.

Leader/pastors tend to seek specific criteria by which their administration will be judged. Among the factors they commonly insert into the review process are the following:

- ✓ positive growth in the evangelistic impact of the church;
- ✓ a superior and consistent quality of worship experienced by the congregation;
- ✓ good financial management;
- ✓ an expanded and increasingly capable team of lay leaders;
- ✓ sub-ministries within the church that can identify how lives are being transformed;
- ✓ a broader influence within the life of the broader community;
- ✓ diminished or minimal participant turnover;
- ✓ an emphasis on strategic thinking and development for the future;
- ✓ absence of significant conflict within the congregation;
- ✓ clarity of vision expressed to staff and congregation;
- ✓ widespread ownership of the vision;
- ✓ ministry activity that reflects adherence to the core values of the church;
- ✓ participation in significant alliances with other ministries.

Two important revelations emerge from such criteria. First, it is apparent that true leaders want to be judged according to their ability to facilitate the six pillars of authentic Christian ministry. That seems sensible; after all, if the leader/pastor accomplishes such outcomes, chances are good that the church he/she leads will be healthy, effective and growing. Yet, we find that such factors are rarely utilized during the pastor review process in churches; the use of such factors is one of the distinguishing attributes of highly effective churches.

Second, notice that these criteria reflect a leader/pastor who is operating at the macro level of ministry. A leader who focuses only on numbers will likely fail the review because the factors that produce depth in ministry (true spiritual health) are overlooked in favor of breadth (numbers of people attending, variety in programs). But a leader who emphasizes the core principles, values and behaviors that produce such outcomes is one who builds a strong foundation upon which continual expansion and efficacy may be experienced. In other words, there is no simplistic, shortcut review that will do justice to the efforts of the leader/pastor—or to the ministry health of his/her church.

The ministry success achieved by the leader/pastor depends largely upon his/her ability to develop a growing corps of competent lay leaders.

Every church is limited in its ministry impact by the aggregate capacity of its leaders. Therefore, one of the most significant tasks of the leader/pastor is to invest in developing as many other leaders as can be raised up from the congregation. The leader who is not focused upon expanding the corps of staff and lay leaders weakens his/her own position in the pursuit of the ministry's vision. If, however, the leader devotes substantial resources—time, energy, money, reflection, and other tangible resources—to the development of potential leaders, both the leader and the church come out ahead as a result.

Leadership from the Pews

One of the most impressive—and important—elements of leadership in the highly effective churches is that most of the leadership comes from the laity. Analysts often focus on the abilities of the pastor, but we find that every highly effective church is able to exploit opportunities and overcome obstacles because of the depth of its lay leadership.

Our studies of highly effective churches also underscored another key reality: God has provided His Church with an abundance of leaders. Contrary to the perception reflected by the question asked by many pastors—*Where are the leaders we need to do effective ministry?*—there are literally millions of lay leaders sitting in the pews in the churches across America, anxious to serve by leading.

This goes back to one of the hallmarks of effective pastors: they invest themselves in the lives of congregants who are, at their core, leaders and who desire the opportunity to serve God and His people through leadership. It is the willingness of pastors to identify and nurture the leadership abilities of others that enables them to be effective as pastors.

Highly effective churches also stand out from the pack because they have a lot of people involved in leadership activities. Whether they are serving as program directors, board members, elders, policymakers or some other type of leader, all in the church who feel called to lead are given ample opportunity to respond to that calling and to use their gifts. Statistically, we discovered that on a per capita basis the typical highly effective church has two to three times more laity involved in leadership than is true in the typical American church. In other words, anywhere from 8 to 12 percent of the congregation is serving in a leadership capacity, compared to 3 to 4 percent in the typical church.

Where do all those leaders come from? Never forget that leaders attract other leaders. When a church has a strong leader at the helm, people who have a similar gift gravitate to that church. Why? Leaders like being led by someone who is a competent leader. Our research has shown that within the past couple of years the Christian Church has driven away literally more than 1 million Christians who are gifted leaders. Many of them departed simply because they could not stand being at a

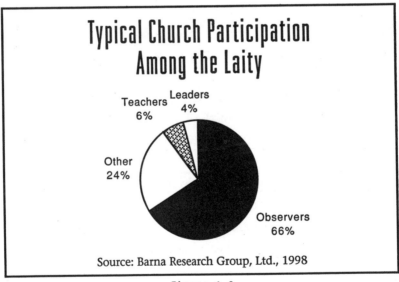

Typical Church Participation Among the Laity

Teachers 6%
Leaders 4%
Other 24%
Observers 66%

Source: Barna Research Group, Ltd., 1998

Figure 1.2

church that had ineffective leadership. Others left because in thousands and thousands of churches a true leader is a threat to the pastor (who, in those cases, is not truly a leader) and is intentionally kept away from leadership duties. Remember, most pastors are not leaders yet they are evaluated according to their ability to effectively lead. Those pastors often assume that the presence of effective lay leaders will inevitably tarnish the pastor's image and job security, placing in jeopardy their livelihood and their platform to do what they enjoy doing—preaching.

Churches with strong leaders also attract additional leaders because the word gets around. There are so few churches that esteem and develop leadership gifts that when such a church emerges, the news spreads like wildfire among Christians with the leadership gift. It is not that they consciously want to go to the same church that every other leader attends, but they are typically so frustrated in other settings that they swiftly move to the place where they are more likely to be appreciated and used most effectively.

A trait of highly effective churches is that they are always on the lookout for more leaders. This, too, is idiosyncratic. Many churches worry that they may become overburdened with leaders, causing the church to be imbalanced. Churches that have a true leader in charge, however, constantly recruit and train leaders because they know a church can never have too many leaders. What do highly effective churches do with such a large cadre of leaders? They turn them loose and let them innovate; they solve existing problems, create new approaches and upgrade the quality of current ministries.

This bottomless appetite for new leaders has several benefits. First, in a culture in which the population is increasingly mobile, every church loses some of its key leaders to relocation. Having a wealth of leaders on hand minimizes the paralysis that could occur as a result of a depleted corps of leaders. Second, the leader/pastor knows that every organization or movement is limited by the capacity of its leadership. Consequently, if the church is going to leave a permanent mark on the community through a growing body of changed lives, it must constantly expand its leadership capacity, which entails both an increased number of leaders and an enhanced quality of leaders. Also, when there is a large team of leaders to draw from, those leaders can be used more appropriately according to their leadership aptitudes and treated more humanely with ample times of rest, refreshment and development.

IDENTIFYING LEADERS

How can you identify the leaders in your midst? The procedures used by highly effective churches included the following:

- talking to the people in the congregation to see whom they perceive to be the most capable leaders;
- observing who is capable of providing strategic direction in response to a ministry challenge or opportunity;
- finding out who provides significant leadership within an occupational arena;
- noting the individuals who demonstrate a keen interest in the vision, plans and development of the ministry;
- listening to the kinds of questions and observations made by congregants to identify people who see the ministry from a leader's perspective;
- examining the results of spiritual gift tests administered among the congregation to discover those to whom God may have given leadership abilities (e.g., the gifts of leadership, shepherding or pastoring are all possibilities);
- identifying the entrepreneurs in the church—the individuals who initiated key ministries, programs or discussions;
- seeking out the mature Christians who are frustrated by the ministry—its pace, organization, focus, performance or untapped potential.

Sometimes determining whether or not an individual is a leader is not as clear-cut as you might imagine—especially if the individual trying to make that determination is not a leader. Sometimes a true leader is not even sure of having what it takes (as exemplified by the reticence to lead shown by David and Moses). To make the assessment easier and more accurate, you might consider using some of the diagnostic tools that have been developed to ascertain a person's leadership potential. Our research has resulted in a comprehensive self-administered diagnostic tool available to churches, the Ministry Leader Profile. This tool helps individuals to answer five crucial questions.

- *Am I called to be a leader?*
  People do not decide that they want to be leaders in ministry; God calls them to that role. This portion of the profile examines the probability of having God's call to ministry leadership.

- *Do I possess the spiritual gift of leadership?*
  God always gives us the tools and resources we need to accomplish the tasks He calls us to achieve. Possessing the spiritual gift of leadership is one of those tools necessary to fulfill His calling to ministry leadership.

- *Is my character the kind that facilitates effective leadership?*
  No leader is perfect. But to be effective, the leader must possess godly character, for it is in the arena of character that Christian leaders are most clearly distinguished from their counterparts who lead in a non-ministry capacity.

• *Do I have the skills that enable leaders to be effective?*
Leaders have natural talents and learned skills that
facilitate leading people. These are their areas of competence; identifying strengths and weaknesses in these
areas enables the individual to lead more effectively.

• *What type of leader am I?*
Every leader possesses one of four leadership aptitudes. Knowing which one he/she has allows them to
focus their efforts for maximum productivity and to
surround themselves with a team of leaders who supplement their ability with complementary leadership
aptitudes.

Other evaluation tools may also prove to be useful. Those
include the Role Preference Inventory, the Personal Profile
System and the Leadership Practices Inventory.[3]

HANDLING LEADERS

Simply acknowledging that someone has been called and gifted to be a ministry leader is not enough. Highly effective
churches go beyond the mere identification of those individuals to a critical second step: developing the leadership abilities
of those people.

The most effective churches in the nation usually create
their own leadership procedures. Our exploration of such procedures shows that they have the following qualities:

• *Every leader is expected to be involved in a*
permanent learning process.
Leadership is evolutionary—and therefore so is the
preparation for effective leadership.

• *The development process is customized to address specific needs of the individual.*

While there are some common lessons and experiences from which all leaders will profit, the most beneficial development is that which addresses the needs and idiosyncrasies of a person. Churches often create these customized plans to reflect the learning style of the persons being developed, the leadership aptitudes they possess, their levels of leadership capacity and their experience.

• *The leadership process is multifaceted.*

None of the churches we studied that effectively develop their leaders relies solely upon classroom or lecture experiences. The most effective programs incorporate a vast array of experiences to grow their leaders.

• *Each leader is immediately incorporated into a team leadership process.*

Because great leadership is always team-based leadership, training is enhanced by placing the leaders in a team-oriented environment. Most of the churches we studied strike a balance between individualized development and team-based activity. Teams are not optional in these ministries; they are the standard vehicle through which one exhibits and refines his/her leadership talents.

• *Constructive evaluation is constantly provided.*

People grow best when they know what is expected of them and how well they are meeting expectations. The most effective churches communicate the standards to which a leader will be held and then provide them with consistent feedback as to how well they are satisfying those standards. Accountability is one of the differentiating points between churches that maintain great leadership and those that experience erratic quality and high turnover of leadership.[4]

Among the advantages churches gain by creating their own training process is the ability to contextualize the training to their own culture. This does not mean that these churches exclude standardized training provided by other organizations or through the use of published resources. Almost all of them integrate some external resources or procedures into their training mix (e.g., seminars, videotapes, books or curriculum created by other organizations). However, because each ministry has a unique vision and culture and those must be related to the core values of the ministry, conceiving a unique approach to leadership development helps to maintain the distinctive nature of the church.

DEPLOYING LEADERS INTELLIGENTLY

Effective churches have also learned that a single leader can't provide all of the leadership required within a church. Our research has identified four different but complementary aspects of leadership that must be provided for a group of people to maximize their progress and influence. Those four unique aspects are known as *dominant leadership aptitudes*. We found that even the greatest leaders usually possess just one of the four aptitudes. That does not mean they are incomplete or incompetent leaders; it is simply a recognition that leadership is so demanding and complex that no one individual can do all aspects of leadership to perfection. (This may be one of the ways that God keeps leaders humble, by impressing upon them their inadequacy to "do it all" even though their skills and gifts are enormously valuable to the ministry.)

The implication of leaders having just one dominant leadership aptitude is that effective leaders must be team players. To get the job done completely and with excellence they must work with a team of leaders who have complementary leadership aptitudes as well as develop work teams comprising people with complementary gifts and abilities to facilitate effective ministry. This perspective means that churches cannot provide generic leadership training and then assume "a leader is a leader." Just as we know that every preacher has his/her own style and unique communication abilities, the same is true for leaders. If the goal of the church is to succeed, it must set up its leaders for success. To do so the church must maximize the gifts and abilities of a leader while compensating for any weaknesses by relying on the efforts of team members who have strengths in those areas of leadership.

A very gratifying outcome of this understanding that one person cannot provide all the leadership a church requires is that people do not think of a church as "Pastor Smith's church." The congregation comes to recognize that Pastor Smith is integral to the health of the church—but also that he, alone, is not responsible for the positive developments happening within that Body of believers. The humility factor at such churches is much healthier than is typical.

THE TEAM CONCEPT

The emphasis placed upon teamwork at these churches is not coincidental. Many of these churches have a high-profile, charismatic leader at the helm, but the reason these churches have grown strong and remained healthy is because they do not rely solely on the extraordinary gifts of a superstar. The church thrives because it has created organic, flexible teams that are responsive to the vision, values and strategy of the ministry.

One of the more interesting findings from my research has been that many small churches appear to have what it takes to become larger, more impactful ministries—but they never realize that potential. Why? Often it is because the leaders of the church are unwilling to recognize their leadership limitations and therefore to work in leadership teams. In other words, such a church is held back by the restricted leadership capacity of those serving in leadership positions. Until those leaders acknowledge and address their own abilities and liabilities, the church will never get beyond its current level of ministry impact.

Teams are most effective when they are created in response to a shared commitment to a specified outcome. Too often churches develop teams on the basis of pre-existing friendships, scheduling convenience or church politics. Teams are useful when there is mutual dependence among the members because they understand that their cooperation creates synergy; they can accomplish more by working together than by working solo. The teams that gain ground for the kingdom are the ones based on purposeful productivity—that is, the individuals on the team are together because their combination of skills, gifts and talents unlocks opportunities that would otherwise go unexploited.

If you want to make the most of the teams you develop at your church, make sure the team understands its purpose clearly (in light of the vision for ministry). Team members have a keen awareness of the strengths and weaknesses they bring to the team and they are willing to handle complex tasks in a cooperative manner. Moreover, relationships that evolve among team members stem from their mutual ownership of the ministry's vision and a desire to deploy their personal competence for the good of the ministry.

IT ALL STARTS WITH LEADERSHIP

In conclusion, let me divulge one other important lesson from our research on leadership in effective churches. You can overcome many deficiencies in a church's ministry and organization, but *you cannot compensate for the lack of good leadership.* Nothing will cripple or even destroy a church more completely than the absence of effective leadership. Many of the highly effective churches throughout America have learned this lesson the hard way. If you can learn from their mistakes, you may be able to avoid the same hardships they endured years ago because of their disregard for the paramount significance of leadership in the ministry.

NOTES
1. Barna, George. *The Second Coming of the Church* (Nashville, TN: Word Books, 1998), p. 106.
2. Ibid., chapter 3.
3. For information regarding the acquisition of these resources see chapter 12 of *The Second Coming of the Church,* George Barna, Word Books, Nashville, TN, 1998. Another valuable resource about methods of leader development is *Learning to Lead,* Jay Conger, Jossey-Bass Publishers, San Francisco, CA, 1992.
4. Additional information on the 10 steps that effective churches incorporate into their development programs can be derived from a live audio presentation by George Barna entitled "Developing Leaders for Ministry," available from the Barna Research Group (1-800-55-BARNA).

STRUCTURING THE CHURCH FOR IMPACT

One of the least appealing activities for many ministry leaders is creating form and structure within the organization they run. Identifying roles, creating systems that facilitate growth, establishing a viable corporate culture, instituting policies—this is not the stuff that most leader/pastors live for! However, every great leader we have studied—from corporate CEOs to successful entrepreneurs to noteworthy leader/pastors— understands that unless he/she designs the structure of their organization appropriately, he/she has hindered the potential of that entity. Developing structure may be a boring or personally taxing venture, but it is one whose benefits justify the investment in the process.

Highly effective churches cannot be agencies of transformation unless they are structured to facilitate effectiveness. Since every church has a different vision, different resources and different ministry opportunities, the exact nature of the structure and operational mode differs. But, again, highly effective churches had some important common traits regarding structure.

Participation Matters

Highly effective churches agree that ministry is not the domain of spectators; it must be populated by activists. Rather than allow (much less facilitate) people to simply come, watch, and give money at the ministry events, leaders at great churches make it clear that you cannot be part of the real church unless you get involved in ministry. From the first time a newcomer visits the church, he/she discovers a core expectation: Active involvement in receiving ministry services (e.g., education, relationships, worship) as well as providing ministry (e.g., volunteering, donating, praying) is essential. These churches aggressively combat a spectator mentality among the people who attend.

Toward that end, a common strategy of these congregations is to identify people visiting the church for the first time and to inform them that the church will prove to be beneficial only if they are willing to get involved right away. To avoid scaring away new believers, non-believers or those who are more introverted or cautious about commitments, these churches have developed ways of softening the pitch and identifying non-threatening means of involvement. However, the core message of their exhortation is clear: get involved or find another place. They communicate this message through the written materials given to visitors regarding the church (e.g., introductory brochures) as well as through the conversations that visitors have with church representatives. The leader/pastor typically encourages everyone in the church to continue to participate in ministry through various comments or principles mentioned during the announcements, the sermon, the prayers and other public utterances made during the weekend service.

A related strategy for promoting constant ministry involvement is to decentralize the decision-making process. One of the most amazing revelations from my research was that in the typical church, the pastor is intimately involved in most, if not all, of the ministry's decisions. (Yes, control is a major problem in the typical American church.) In the highly effective churches, however, the leader/pastor has the final say on all of the major ministry decisions, but is literally uninvolved in the vast majority of decisions made in the ministry.

These leader/pastors are so secure in the capacity and ability of the staff and lay leaders in the church that they delegate enormous amounts of responsibility and authority to large numbers of people. "If I have done my job properly," one of the highly effective pastors explained, "then there are many people in the congregation who are capable of providing leadership that is consistent with our vision and values. And that means that I can focus on other aspects of the ministry with the assurance that things will run smoothly without my butting in to every ministry we have going. It is freeing for me, exhilarating for others involved in our ministry and very beneficial for the church since it multiplies our ministry capacity well beyond my own limited reach."

The tangible outcomes of decentralization and delegation are evident. Highly effective churches are able to respond rapidly to crises and opportunities that emerge. They are able to touch a greater number of lives. And they are capable of developing and sustaining a broader range of ministry services and programs because of their commitment to incorporating everyone into the process. Naturally, this is not simply a matter of letting everyone do anything they please; there is a huge need for excellent management of the ministry. However, it seems that letting go of control is the major hurdle for most churches; efficiently managing the activities that result from the release of control and the consequent empowerment of believers is an easier task to accomplish.

MINIMIZING PAID STAFF

One of the secrets to achieving universal ministry participation is to eliminate the possibility of congregational dependence upon staff. In tens of thousands of multiple-staff churches, the staff members are viewed as the ministers; when ministry must be done, it is assigned to staff who must then cajole congregants to get involved as necessary. In fact, our research indicates that most Protestant pastors see growth in the number of paid staff as an indicator of church health and good leadership.

The leader/pastors of highly effective churches possess an entirely different perspective. Their objective is to facilitate as much ministry as humanly possible through the efforts of the congregation, with as few full-time, paid ministers as possible. For example, one church we studied had eight full-time people serving a church with more than 6,000 adults attending on a weekly basis. Another had more than 4,000 adults at the weekly worship events with a full-time paid staff of 10. Compare these proportions to the national norm among churches of 300 or more, which seems to be approximately one full-time paid staff person for every 75-100 adults attending the church regularly.

Highly effective churches are always suspicious of a growing payroll. While they understand that increased staff may facilitate productive ministry, they also recognize that increased reliance upon staff can quickly turn a movement of faith into a religious bureaucracy. These churches typically prefer "guerrilla ministry tactics" to the predictable and smoother ministry that may result from paying full-time professionals to get the job done. "If the people don't really own the ministry, using staff as surrogates to do their work for them doesn't really get us where we need to be," explained one pastor. "I rely upon full-time staff to help us get things done around here, but if we count on them too much or too often, the laity can get spiritually lazy very quickly. I want them to grow, and watching somebody else do ministry is not a good growth strategy. If they're excited about what we're doing, then they need to translate that excitement into ground-level ministry activity. It may not look as pretty or have the same philosophical grounding as what my staff would do, but it helps us to be more ministry minded."

How do they accomplish this minimum-staff/maximum-ministry magic? I have observed six factors that are commonly involved:

- *The standard of expectations is raised.*
  "To be part of this church, you have to be involved in ministry"; there is no uncertainty about expectations, nor any value associated with "spectator Christianity."

- *Opportunities for laziness and dependence are removed.*
  The church hires comparatively few full-time staff and their roles are very carefully defined. This puts the responsibility for ministry squarely upon the shoulders of the congregants.

- *Adequate training is provided for volunteers.*
  Continued participation relies upon positive experiences. Therefore these churches help congregants understand

their giftedness, give them appropriate training, and direct them to appropriate ministry options.

- *Control of the ministry is released to the laity.*
  The role of the leader/pastor is to provide vision, motivation, mobilization, direction and resources to the laity. The role of other staff is to reinforce motivation, facilitate team building and disseminate resources strategically. Ultimately, because the ministry wins or loses on the basis of what the laity do, the laity must have control over the ministry.

- *Efforts of lay ministers are reinforced.*
  Celebrating the hard work and ministry successes of lay ministers both publicly and privately goes a long way toward enhancing their commitment and self-assurance.

- *Skills and resources of paid staff are used very judiciously.*
  Leadership and management dovetail to use the time and energy invested by staff for maximum ministry impact.

When highly effective churches do hire full-time staff, even their process strays from the norm. More often than not, they hire one of their lay ministers—often as a part-time employee, then perhaps eventually as a full-time minister. Their reasoning is simple and logical. When you hire from the outside, you can never really tell what you'll be getting. When you hire from the inside, there is less guesswork involved. You know the person's strengths and weaknesses; they understand and have accepted the church's vision for ministry; they know the terrain—the people, the structure, the history, the community, the church. You know their faith-maturity level; you have experienced their capabilities in action; and you know if they are compatible with existing congregants, leaders and staff. Such experience and knowledge never totally eliminates the risk associated with ushering a lay person into a full-time ministry position. Perhaps the most impressive testimony to this hiring process, though, is that highly effective churches have a lower staff turnover rate than do other churches. This is at least partly attributable to hiring people who were formerly lay ministers at the church.

STRUCTURING MINISTRIES TO MEET CHANGING NEEDS

One strategy that has worked wonders for highly effective churches is their commitment to changing the church's structure and policies as often as necessary to reflect new insights, needs and opportunities. Perhaps this approach seems like common sense. It is, but as Mark Twain once wrote, "common sense ain't." The proof is that most churches evaluate ministry needs and opportunities in light of the ability of the church's existing structure and policies to address those needs and opportunities. It's the tail-wagging-the-dog syndrome, yet thousands of churches operate in that fashion.

Imagine the practical implications of a structure-follows-ministry approach:

- *Flexibility in Changing Ministry Policies*
  A ministry policy is valid as long as it is biblically defensible and facilitates effective operation. At the first sign that a policy inhibits ministry that conforms to the church's vision, that policy is strenuously reevaluated—and, more often than not, changed. Few effective churches lose sleep over policy changes; such transitions are standard operating procedures and are accomplished quickly and without fuss.

- *Flexibility in Changing Staff*
  Staffing shifts from time to time to reflect the changing capacity of the congregation. Given a ministry philosophy in which staff is thought to be peripheral rather than central, and in which the purpose of staff is to support the work of lay ministers, changes in staffing are not unusual or unsettling.

- *Flexibility in Ending or Restructuring a Ministry*
  Every ministry program must constantly justify its existence through measures of life transformation because every program is considered expendable. The criteria for viability hinge upon life transformation, not history, politics or popularity. It is not uncommon for a highly effective church to scrap a very popular program or a ministry with a long history in the church solely because the resources consumed by the program (e.g., space, church image, leadership and teaching capacity, funds) cannot be justified by the apparent impact of the program.

Leaders/pastors at highly effective churches drive the process of *challenging the value* of existing ministries, programs, policies and practices. They train their fellow leaders to recognize that every program and policy has a life cycle and that eventually every program and policy must be updated to reflect environmental changes. Killing a program or altering a policy is not a sign of defeat—it is a mark of vitality. The refusal to address this reality spells danger for a church. A church where the structure drives the ministry is one in which ministry opportunities will be regularly lost.

Highly effective churches can take this bold approach to change because they have decentralized, delegated, released control and empowered the people for ministry. Structure, in such settings, is substantially less important than firm ownership of the ministry's vision and values. Once the vision and values become the driving force behind operational decisions, policies and programs are of relatively less consequence anyway. Change—and even unpredictability—becomes a way of life in such ministries. But it is the ability to adapt to circumstances without fear of reprisal or without anxiety about policy limitations that enables a church to remain responsive to the opportunities God provides.

PLANNED GROWTH THAT IS REASONABLE

Many of the keenest insights highly effective churches have learned were discovered through harsh reality: trial and error, abject failure, unexpected victories. One of their most important structural insights is one that most of them stumbled onto: *You must limit your annual numerical growth.*

I have been amazed at how perplexing, agonizing or infuriating this notion is to most pastors.

Leader/pastors at highly effective churches drive the process of *challenging the value* of existing ministries,

programs, policies and practices. Killing a program or altering a policy is not a sign of defeat—it is a mark of vitality.

When I encourage them to think in terms of limiting their growth, the first question that comes to their minds is: *Why would I ever want to do that? Jesus called us to reach the entire world, not to lay back and reach just a small portion of it.*

True enough. But Jesus also expects us to be wise. That means learning from our own mistakes and from those of others in ministry. Clearly, one of the lessons is that attracting large numbers of people to a church is not hard to do. Getting them to come back, week after week, and ensuring that they are growing spiritually is something else. That is precisely why highly effective churches strive to have an annual growth rate of no more than 15 percent. Across the board, we found that when appealing, well-led, vision-focused churches grew by more than 15 percent, it created problems such as high turnover, inefficient use of resources and breakdowns in support systems. In essence, growing by more than 15 percent per year creates significant assimilation problems.

Our research on congregational dynamics suggests that growing by more than 15 percent per year puts untenable stress on a church. First, the congregation cannot appropriately absorb more people than that through supportive, healthy relationships. Many who are attracted to the church therefore drop out after a relatively brief period of satisfaction and raised hopes. Second, few churches are capable of placing 15 percent more people into meaningful ministry after providing them with proper guidance, training and resources. Churches that grow by more than 15 percent generally add a wealth of spectator Christians, thereby negating the strengths gained by building a body of active lay ministers. Third, when a congregation grows too quickly it usually fails to evaluate the development of newcomers adequately. The result is that too many of these new adherents fail to grow spiritually—and nobody knows or cares.

How can you limit growth without rejecting spiritually needy people? Here are some of the methods used by highly effective churches.

- *Periodically preach a series of "hard truth" messages.*
These are sermons where the high cost of true discipleship is clearly and forcefully articulated by the preacher. One pastor of a highly effective church noted that whenever the church's growth curve quickens, he knows it's time for such a series. "I figure they have underestimated what the Christian faith requires. I find that after a four or five-week series of these tough messages, our attendance drops by several hundred people. It's not that I don't love those people or don't want our ministry to influence them. I simply don't want people coming here because it's the hot church in town or for other inappropriate reasons. If they're serious about growing in Christ, we'll do everything humanly possible to support them. But they need to count the cost of discipleship."

- *Set higher and higher standards of quality in ministry.*
People are attracted to receiving quality—but many are not as willing to invest themselves in serving at such high levels of ministry quality. For the church to expect everyone to minister to the utmost of their abilities—and to accept nothing less—frustrates many people who are willing to take from the best, but not to give their best to others.

- *Limit program involvement to the maximum level at which the church can provide excellence.*
Many highly effective churches limit the number of children allowed in Sunday School classes so that the

children enrolled receive the attention and quality of teaching they deserve. While some people view this as insensitive or harsh, highly effective churches recognize that spreading limited resources too thin merely dilutes and ultimately destroys effective ministry.

- *Modify marketing efforts based upon growth projections.* Highly effective churches are not beholden to attendance or membership figures. They do monitor such figures, though, so that they can adjust their ministry efforts to ensure that the church remains focused on quality rather than quantity. If the church experiences a growth spurt during a particular period of time, ministry plans may be quickly altered to reduce the probability of continued, snowballing growth in the forthcoming time period.

- *Work cooperatively with other churches to introduce new-comers to other congregations that might be more effective at meeting their needs.*
  People often start attending a highly effective church because of the church's reputation for quality and commitment to people's growth. However, sometimes the effective church is not the church in town that is best geared to meeting the unique needs of the incoming individual. Naturally, an effective church has worked hard to be effective; it would never intentionally do anything that would undermine its positive impact. But, when visitors come to the church with serious needs and high hopes, everyone is better off if the church can assess the real needs of the visitor (spiritual, relational, emotional) and suggest a church that might be better suited to serving and assimilating such a person.

The preference for growing deep rather than broad ultimately strengthens the church and enables it to continue to grow both deep and broad over the course of time. The insistence upon quality rather than quantity is what ultimately enables some highly effective churches to grow unusually large.

DEMAND ACCOUNTABILITY

No organization becomes and remains successful unless it constantly scrutinizes its own performance. Continual self-examination is a hallmark of highly effective churches. Rather than avoid the tough questions, they invite them. Instead of silencing critics, they encourage them to voice their concerns (as long as it is done in a positive, constructive manner). While many churches deny change on the grounds that the congregation is growing numerically or that the people are pleased with how things are going, highly effective churches never rest on their past or present performance because they are driven by God's vision for the ministry's future. The vision invariably challenges the church to blaze new trails and accomplish more than it has already achieved.

In my study of highly effective churches there have been four factors that stand out as critical to making accountability work. First, the leader/pastor must be a relentless champion of accountability. If he/she constantly promotes the value and necessity of self-assessment (both individually and as a body of believers), then the congregation will eventually embrace that call to excellence. Not surprisingly I found the converse to be true as well: If a leader/pastor does not champion accountability, the church never seriously calls for it and the consequence is a church where activity is mistaken for purposeful ministry.

Second, the criteria used for evaluation are of paramount importance. None of the highly effective churches I examined relied solely upon the typical standards such as attendance, membership, budget, number of compliments on the sermon or number of ministry programs and events. Although such measures were taken into account, these churches created unique ways of measuring change. In order to determine change in people's lives these churches rely upon honest relationships as the means of collecting the information needed to arrive at a judgment about the state of the church.

Third, accountability is not a closed-ended, once-a-year process that can be completed in a two-week period of energetic self-examination. The highly effective churches constantly reflect on their status and progress and perpetually strive to improve. Over the long haul this becomes an ingrained part of the corporate culture—ministry habits. The leader/pastor remains a champion of accountability, but the congregation accepts the challenge to continually implement the process. Once the people overcome the fear of evaluation and anxiety regarding change, the process of self-examination becomes accepted for its true value—*a means to greater obedience to Christ.*

Fourth, when deficiencies or shortcomings are discovered, the leaders are completely committed to making changes that will facilitate effective ministry. It is one thing to recognize the need for change and to acknowledge that need; making the required changes is another matter. How do these churches get their people to willingly embrace change? Many congregants are motivated by watching their leaders model such behavior. Others are encouraged to take bold steps because the church has reinforced the value of self-examination and the role of change in growth. Still others were willing to break from the comfortable and try something different because the church had highlighted the growth achieved through past transitions. And, of course, all of the effective churches made openness to purposeful and strategic change a centerpiece of their ministry philosophy.

As with every church, even the highly effective churches in America often stumble in their efforts to become efficient facilitators of life transformation. Sometimes they waste resources, they work within convoluted lines of authority, they invest too much control in the hands of the wrong individuals or too few individuals or they go on a hiring spree and wind up with a bloated staff.

But in the end these churches teach us an invaluable lesson about ministry structure. No matter what structure you adopt for your ministry, it is a structure that must serve you well today, but one that should be expected to do no more than act as a launching pad for the structure that will serve you best tomorrow. Structure exists to foster ministry impact, not to impair it. Therefore constant self-assessment is a necessity, but what you evaluate, how you interpret the evaluation data and how you administer change will determine the health and growth potential of your ministry. You only improve that which you measure, and the results of those measurements are meaningful only if your measurement criteria coincide with your vision, your values and a passion for excellence.

NOTE

1. This is most appropriate for churches of 150 or more adult attenders. The maximum strategic growth rate may be different for smaller churches.

BUILDING LASTING, SIGNIFICANT RELATIONSHIPS

A recurrent theme through-out the history of the Church is that of creating a loving, caring community. The story of the Early Church recounted in Acts emphasizes the importance of relationships among believers. Jesus' ministry was a model of commitment to fellow believers: He did everything with the family of faith; He ate, talked, traveled and ministered with His disciples. He did more than simply talk about love for others; Jesus personally modeled it and consistently arranged situations and opportunities for His faith-circle to deepen and demonstrate their love for each other.

Developing a Relational Philosophy

When you interview the pastors of highly effective churches, a common theme that emerges is the importance of people's relationships.

> For years my personal focus as a pastor was to make sure people understood Christianity. My energy was devoted to my sermons, and in meetings with church leaders I was the champion of Christian education. Over time I realized that what I had created was a group of sinners with head knowledge. I'm not knocking Bible knowledge—that's very important. But over the last decade my philosophy has changed dramatically. Today, I'm more concerned about who we are than about what we know. And the best way for us to become the faith community that Christ intends is to live in intimate relationship with Him and with other Christians. Our church is much more tuned in to living the faith together than to memorizing the faith in isolation.

Highly effective churches are more than just friendly congregations. In our surveys we often find that church leaders believe that a church has gone the distance if it is overtly friendly—at least on Sunday mornings. But our broader research efforts have discovered that what makes a church secure and stable is not mere friendliness but true concern, compassion and caring for others. Surprisingly few churches have focused on these deeper aspects of community.

Perhaps part of the dilemma relates to the goal that churches have for the relationships fostered within the congregation. Most churches give surprisingly little thought to how relationships develop in the church and what the ideal contours of those relationships would be. Even the recent energy devoted by churches to creating extensive small groups or cell groups amounts to little more than a means of retaining attenders through relational ties.

Highly effective churches usually identify spiritual renewal as the ultimate goal of the relationships developed within the church network. Their perspective is that believers are to know, love and serve each other—just as we are to know, love and serve God Himself. To do so requires a purposeful and long-term commitment to relationships with other believers. The church, as the unifying organization, merely becomes the repository through which serious faith-based relationships emerge and are nurtured. Consequently, the local church can be defined not through its programs, buildings, events, staff or teaching, but through the cumulative web of relationships that have been initiated and maintained among those who associate with that organization.

One pastor of a highly effective church stated it in different terms.

Our church is not the group of people who show up Sunday morning to attend a weekly religious event. The real church is the people who are emotionally connected by their mutual and stated love for Christ and by their commitment to each other because of Christ. One of my goals as the leader of this church is to enlarge the circle of people who are emotionally connected to the spiritual heartbeat of this body of people.

When we first implemented our relational ministry strategy five or six years ago, maybe 10 percent of the congregation was really operating as a community of faith. Almost everyone was coming here for the preaching or other services and programs we provided. Today, I estimate that about 60 to 70 percent are here because of their relationships with other people who are very serious about their Christianity. The Sunday services have almost become dispensable. What is indispensable now is our root system, the friendships and accountability relationships that permeate this place. The other 30 or 40 percent need to come along and become part of that process, because that's where the real church resides. The services are, in some ways, just an excuse for the real church to get together. Most of the real ministry occurs off campus, through relationships—and, frankly, I never hear about it unless I ask.

ESTABLISHING RELATIONAL PRIORITIES

Building a church based on relationships, however, does not mean that every Christian should befriend everyone he/she meets; that is unrealistic. Instead, many highly effective churches encourage their people to develop "intentional relationships." This phrase is designed to affirm the inability to intimately know and love everyone in the world. Therefore, believers are encouraged to intentionally create "relational priorities."

What is the single most important relationship a Christian can have? It is his/her relationship with Jesus Christ. Our schedule and allocation of personal resources (e.g., energy, consideration) should therefore reflect the top priority of that relationship. Our priorities should be clear:

- Christ is first in all matters;
- family is second;
- relationships with other believers, in particular our church family, is third;

• those outside the community of faith—nonbelievers with whom we work—live next to and encounter from day to day.

Being lower on this hierarchy does not mean we should treat those people with less love or respect. We don't necessarily love these people less in terms of how we treat them. Our behavior simply reflects that we have to apportion our limited emotional resources in the most reasonable manner. Scripture indicates that the four-step priority scheme promoted by many highly effective churches is appropriate.[1]

I have found that many pastors operating in a less effective church environment struggle with this concept of prioritizing time and resources. Common retorts include: "But Jesus called us to reach the lost!" or "Christians should not discriminate against anyone because of where they are in their faith journey; we should love everyone equally." Perhaps the notion of establishing a pecking order in one's relationships has caused you some discomfort or has raised similar questions in your own mind.

I am more convinced than ever that this relational priorities principle is a vital distinctive of highly effective churches. Why? Because when churches focus their energy on priority relationships, they become strategic. Think of it this way: If you try to create meaningful relationships with all people, whenever and wherever opportunities arise, you become an emotional victim. In essence, because there are no boundaries to your efforts, your relational energy is accessible but compromised; your impact, rather than concentrated and significant, becomes dissipated and marginal. If, instead, you intentionally seek to develop positive and productive relationships based upon significant factors for the purpose of mutual spiritual growth, your faith remains central, meaningful and influential. But if you allow circumstances to

Leaders must

establish relational

priorities and think

strategically

in building friendships.

Otherwise, if you try

to create meaningful

relationships with

all people,

whenever and wherever

opportunities arise,

you become an

emotional victim.

dictate the people with whom you spend time and personal emotional resources, you will lose the strategic ministry impact you could have achieved. There will be exceptions to this rule, but the central reality is that random relationships rarely result in strategic spiritual gain.

Note that highly effective churches also teach their people that it is not acceptable to focus on relationships with Christ, family and fellow believers to the exclusion of outsiders. Every Christian has a responsibility to connect with nonbelievers in ways that allow for "lifestyle evangelism" as well as more direct discussion about faith matters. Highly effective churches are unique in that they prod their people to invest larger proportions of their emotional resources in the most important relationships while still investing some resources in other relationships that are significant but of relatively lesser importance. It is a question of balance. It is also, in the minds of highly effective churches, a matter of stewardship.

RELATIONSHIPS FOSTER GROWTH

To underscore the importance of relationships, highly effective congregations place the vast bulk of their numerical-growth efforts into relational marketing. Instead of seeking to attract visitors to the church through impersonal means such as direct mail advertising, radio commercials, TV ads or highway billboards, these churches seek numerical growth by having the regular attendees personally invite friends to show up with them. Sometimes this is facilitated through special events such as concerts, theatrical presentations or family outings. The most important element of this approach, though, is the impact of *personal touch.*

Our research throughout the past decade has shown that this emphasis upon relationships has become increasingly important in attracting the unchurched to attend a church. If the unchurched want a great event, there are thousands of organizations that can put on a better show than the typical church. If the unchurched simply want to be in the presence of other people, there are ample opportunities to have such experiences, usually in much less threatening environments. But the Church is unique in that it is intended to be a community—not just an aggregation of unrelated people simultaneously seeking their own benefit, but a group of individuals with a common purpose and a set of explicit relational parameters where true relationships are meant to flourish.

Thus, when highly effective churches welcome a newcomer to the community of faith, the "stick rate" (the probability of retention) of those people is higher than the norm. This is explained primarily by one factor: The visitor came because of a pre-existing personal relationship with someone who was part of the church, and he/she returned because of the emotional safety and security visitors experience, facilitated by that initial relationship. Visitors immediately feel they are actually part of the church because they are already relationally tied in to the church.

There is another factor that has helped many highly effective churches to foster a relational ministry: They assume that many people do not know how to build a lasting, positive relationship. In response to this realization, these churches develop procedures to help their people discover the ways to accomplish this outcome. Some effective churches encourage their leaders to mentor people on relational practices. Other effective churches offer courses on how to build and maintain friendships. Many of these churches create frequent events geared to furthering burgeoning relationships. Sometimes those are family events; other times they are general social events for specific niches within the church family. The serious commitment to facilitating relationships is one of the secrets to growth and satisfaction within these churches.

MODELING MEANINGFUL RELATIONSHIPS

Some believers do not automatically build meaningful relationships with other people in the church simply because the leadership verbally espouses a philosophy of relational ministry. One of the most powerful antecedents for a congregation learning to live according to relational priorities is having the church's most visible leaders model that lifestyle.

There is a palpable difference between a church where the senior leaders devote serious amounts of time to their relationship with Christ and those churches where such a commitment, if it exists, is less obvious. Sometimes the ways in which leaders invest time in their relationship with Christ is obvious: attendance at spiritual seminars, participation in church events, etc. Often, the commitment is implied through the manifestations of that commitment: an overt sense of peace with God, a greater aura of spiritual wisdom, a tendency to seek first God's direction through prayer, extensive biblical knowledge, obvious compassion for needy people, etc.

Similarly, one of the most striking attributes of highly effective churches is that every leader is a "family man" or "family woman" who spends less time and fewer evenings in church meetings, specifically so that more non-work hours can be spent with family. They think about the implications of church activities and events on family life before determining the fate of those activities and events. They show honest concern for the health and vitality of others' families through their conversations and decisions. Moreover, one of the most appealing attributes of these leaders is that they truly enjoy being with their families— and their ministry decisions reflect that priority.

A CORE BENEFIT OF RELATIONSHIPS

Two decades of research within and concerning the Church have taught me many lessons. First, millions of people return week after week to their church because of the personal relationships they developed there. They remain faithful to a local Body even when the preaching is marginal, the organizational structure is lacking and the church has little to offer outside of Sunday services. The core reason they return each week is because of friendships they have within that church.

One of the foundations of ministry success is *relational consistency.* Highly effective churches do not have to invest oodles of resources in trying to familiarize an endless stream of newcomers with the mission, vision and values of the church because the people who come and visit, stay. Those people stay in the church because of the emotional connections that develop within the congregation. Leaving the church would cut themselves off from "family."

Here is some interesting evidence of the centrality of relationships at highly effective churches: Every year in America, about one out of every five families relocates. Most households move within 25 miles of their previous location. However, we have found that most people who move to a new location will use the transition as an excuse to leave the church they had been attending in favor of another church that is closer to their new home.

When someone attending a highly effective church relocates, however, they are much more likely than average to continue attending the church they had been attending prior to their move. Even though this often means that their commute to the church increases, sometimes by up to 30 minutes each way, most of the relocating households choose to maintain their ties with the church because it had become their spiritual home. Interviews with those individuals reveal that the primary draw is not the preaching, the children's program or the doctrine of the church; the magnet is the relationships that they've cultivated with others in the church.

God made us to be in relationships—with Himself and with other people. Highly effective churches have tapped into this inclination by intentionally addressing every person's need to belong to something special. A church that fosters true community is indeed something special.

NOTE
  1. The research among highly effective churches indicates that this four-step prioritization is not found at every one of these churches. In some congregations additional types of relationships were included in the hierarchy; in other churches the ordering of the priorities differed. The four priorities listed here were the most common approach observed at the highly effective churches studied, but they are clearly not the only ranking that exists.

FACILITATING GENUINE WORSHIP

(4)

Almost every Christian church provides worship experiences for its people. In most cases, the weekly worship service is the ministry centerpiece of the church. In some instances, the worship service is the only real ministry activity of the church.

But America has a worship problem. Our surveys among regular church-going adults indicate that one-third of those people have never experienced God's presence. Half of all regular church-going adults admit that they have not experienced God's presence at any time during the past year. The younger the adult, the more likely they are to state that God is a distant, impersonal reality for them. And even among those who say God's presence was evident to them, most of them say that happened only one or two times throughout the course of the year.

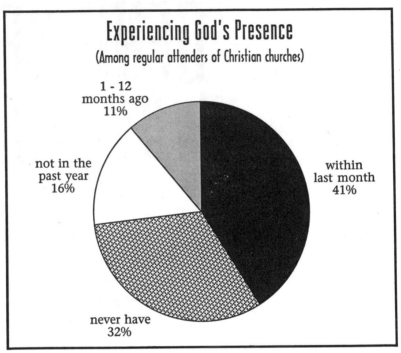

Figure 4.1

How is it possible that a God who so desperately wants to love and be loved by His creatures seems to be in voluntary seclusion? How is it possible that among individuals who make the effort to frequently attend church services—attending an average of more than 25 worship services in the past year—half of them have not experienced God's presence at all in the past 12 months, in spite of desiring that very outcome?

The answers are many, varied and eye opening:

• *No Definition of Worship*
  A majority of adults attending Christian churches

have no idea what worship means. Two out of three cannot provide an appropriate definition or description of worship.

- ### *No Priority of Worship*
A minority of people who regularly attend Christian worship services describe worship as a "top priority" in their lives. It need not be the top priority, but most of them do not even include it among a list of top priorities.

- ### *Wrong Perceptions About Worship*
Millions of adults who frequently attend church believe that the purpose of attending is to have a pleasing experience. There are more people who believe that attending worship services is for personal benefit or pleasure than those who believe worship is what we do for God. "Good worship" is seen as singing songs or hymns we like, hearing a sermon that we understand or rate favorably (either it is comforting, comfortable or helpful) or interacting with friends.

Religious Activity Substitutes for Spiritual Relationships
Many attenders, lacking any understanding about the content or purposes of worship, assume that the routines and rituals that occur in worship services constitute the substance of worship. Consequently, these individuals settle for religious activity rather than a spiritual relationship with God, mistaking ritual for worship.

- ### *Poor Sensitivity to God's Presence*
Many church leaders and pastors think that worship succeeds when it is efficient (smooth transitions dur-

ing the service, inclusion of the various components, completed within the desired time frame). Astoundingly few identify outcomes such as sensitivity to the Holy Spirit, facilitating a worshipful environment or fostering God's presence to be central factors in the value of the worship event.

• *No Desire to Confront Sin*

Avoidance of divine confrontation is a hallmark of American worship. Most churches cringe at the thought of worship as a time when people might address the huge gap between God's holiness and our sinfulness. Rather than allow God to confront us during worship, we instead evaluate worship according to the levels of comfort and professionalism achieved.

The good news is that highly effective churches not only prioritize worship, they have created ways of ensuring that real worship occurs. The procedures I will describe in the remainder of this chapter are approaches that many of them have backed into; often they knew that the quality of worship at their church was lacking, but were not sure how to overcome the problem. Through trial and error they were able to solve their dilemma. The steps they have taken are probably steps that would enhance the quality of worship in any church—including yours.

Defining True Worship

One stumbling block for many churches is in getting their people to possess an accurate understanding of what worship is— and is not. This must be addressed at two levels:

- what does worship mean for the worshiper?
- what does worship mean for those at the church who will be responsible for consistently facilitating true worship?

For the church leaders responsible for enabling people to worship God with all their heart, mind, soul and strength, worship means creating an environment in which people can personally and intimately connect with God to glorify, honor and bless Him. The people who attend a worship service should be ushered into His presence through an intentional effort to make God's presence palpable. For highly effective churches this has meant a reengineering of how the worship service is designed, how it is carried out and how it is evaluated.

The design of the service, which will be discussed at length in subsequent pages, is based upon driving for success (enabling people to experience God in a tangible, practical, but highly spiritual way). Part of the challenge for these churches has been to ensure that those developing or leading the worship event are sensitive to the guidance of the Holy Spirit and willing to follow the Spirit's promptings. In practical terms this means entering the service with a well-conceived agenda of how the service will proceed, but being willing to stray from that agenda if there is a true sense that God would be better honored or served through some alternative effort.

How do highly effective churches evaluate the worship service? Here are a few of the common ways worship times are assessed:

- people are clearly moved—physically, emotionally or intellectually—by the experience: deep questions were answered, dubious behaviors were seriously chal-

lenged, personal faith-commitment level was stirred;
- emotional or physical healing of some discernible nature occurred;
- people are anxious to return to the church for another God-encounter, hoping to again experience the intense joy or fulfillment of that day's encounter;
- worshipers had an undeniable sense of God's presence in their midst;
- individuals experienced a deep need to repent before God;
- there was a willingness to surrender control of their lives and allow God to direct them in a more intimate and pervasive manner;
- the sermon provided a biblical impetus for people to clarify their worldview and to grow holistically.

Indicators not relied upon to assess the worship time in highly effective churches include:

- the number of compliments given to the preacher for the sermon;
- the number of visitors present or the increase in attendance from previous weeks;
- the size of the offering;
- how smoothly the service ran;
- the number of people who appeared to be singing during the congregational hymns and choruses, or the number of people who recited the congregational response during liturgy response times;
- the number of people who came forward or participated in communion;
- how many people appeared to be taking notes during the sermon.

Successful worship is not likely until one understands that worship is not attending an event but is a state of mind and spirit. My conversations about worship with effective church leaders raised two critical matters that were instrumental in the transition from focusing upon filling the sanctuary to focusing upon filling people's hearts with God's Spirit. First, the challenge of true worship is to get people to *obsess on God*. Only when we are completely focused on Him and fully determined to interact with Him in an appropriate way is He honored through our worship. Second, if the church exists for the purpose of facilitating life transformation, that level of life change is not because of anything we do but because of people's ability to truly experience God's presence. Thus motivating people to attend worship to encounter the living God became an obsession of the church leaders.

UNDERSTANDING WORSHIP

Getting Americans to grasp the real meaning of worship is not an easy task. Let's be honest, motivating people to worship something other than self or material possessions is a counter-cultural challenge. Among the two-thirds who attend church services regularly but could not provide a proper definition of worship, some of the more common guesses were that worship is "attending church," "being a church member" and "believing that God exists." The most common answer, though, was "I don't know." We have wandered so far from fundamental spiritual knowledge in our culture that literally tens of millions of people—many of whom have long-term ties with the Christian church—have no clue how to even describe a true spiritual experience.

Highly effective churches often incorporate one or more of the following approaches into their efforts to educate the congregation about worship:

• *Establish that worship is about our focusing on God,*
  not God focusing on us.
  Most adults attend worship services with one dominant person on their mind: themselves. Before people
  can worship God, they must see how crucial it is to
  focus their attention on the Being they have allegedly
  come to worship.

• *Provide adults with a compelling reason*
  to engage in worship.
  The majority of adults now attending churches are
  Boomers and Busters—that is, people in their twen-
  ties, thirties and forties. Among the characteristics of
  these generations is that they do not follow traditional or expected patterns of activity unless they have a
  good reason to do so. Highly effective churches often
  challenge younger adults to articulate why they go to
  church and, upon discovering reasons that have nothing to do with worship, refocus the conversation on
  the meaning of worship and related reasons that justify worship. Among the reasons suggested are that
  the Bible commands us to worship Him; He deserves
  our worship; our worship gives God pleasure; if we
  truly love Him, we should be willing to honor Him
  through worship.

• *Explain how worship is both an attitude and an action.*
  Most people are used to thinking of worship as something that they do (or, unfortunately, a place they go
  or an event they attend). Highly effective churches
  teach their people that worship is both an action (i.e.,
  engaging in efforts to intentionally glorify God) and

an attitude. An attitude of worship implies that we feel privileged to give God glory and honor, that we are humbled by the ability to experience and interact with Him, that we acknowledge our own sinfulness in contrast to His purity, and that we view worshiping God to be one of the most incredible opportunities we may experience in life.

- *Facilitate the ability to become intimate with God.* Interestingly, our research suggests that many people may struggle in achieving intimacy with God because they have never had true intimacy with people on earth and therefore are uncomfortable or unfamiliar with such closeness. Churches have had success leading people to understand intimacy with God by starting at square one in this process—defining what intimacy means and accomplishes, then moving forward progressively to the point at which they are able experience that depth of connection with God.

- *Encourage people to come to the worship event prepared to worship.* Relatively few adults—just one out of three church attenders believe that preparation for worship prior to going to a church service is important. Fewer than half as many actually make any effort to get themselves mentally or spiritually ready before arriving at the worship event. Millions of adults consider their attendance at the event to be ample proof of their commitment to worship. However, a large majority of adults do not enter the worship event with a mind or heart that is focused on God or tuned into worship. The result is that worship leaders exhaust a lot of precious time and energy trying to direct people's undivided attention to God. When people take the time to read the Bible, pray or engage in other exercises designed to prepare them for worship prior to arriving at the event site, worship is much more likely to occur.

• *Place the burden of success in worship upon the individual, not the institution.*
How many people attend church services almost daring the church to get them to worship? Highly effective churches have overcome this pressure by placing the responsibility for worship on the worshiper, rather than upon the church as it attempts to facilitate that experience. This twist encourages people to have a clear sense of why they are seeking to worship, what worship is, to feel responsible to be prepared for the experience and to release the church from responsibility for "making" them worship. When they attend a church to worship in the presence of other believers, worship is a corporate experience—but worship will only occur for them if they accept the responsibility for making worship happen and commit to initiating that process in their lives.

Once people understand what worship is about, why they would bother to worship God, and who bears the responsibility for making worship happen, the chances of authentic worship occurring are hugely increased. Without taking this first step and ensuring that people "get it," worship services will always be a hit-or-miss prospect.

RELATING TO JESUS CHRIST

One of the more insidious obstacles to church-based worship is the fact that, on average, nearly half of the people who attend worship services at Protestant churches are not Christian. By this I mean that they have never made an intentional commitment to Christ that included a confession of their sins and that serves as the basis for their belief that they will have eternal salvation.[1] I mention this in regard to worship because my research indicates that if a person does not have a personal relationship with God through Jesus Christ, the chance of his/her truly worshiping God is slim.

Consequently, highly effective churches are committed to confronting non-Christian attenders with the opportunity to embrace Christ as their Savior. (The chapter on strategic evangelism describes how this is done.) Not surprisingly, the proportion of Christians attending highly effective churches is much higher than is found in Christian churches across the board.

Whether intentional or not, this commitment to having professing Christians in the congregation has had a cleansing effect on the worship experience. Consider what happens when you have a congregation of people who have come together to worship God. Not only do relatively few of them understand what worship is, but half of them don't even know the deity they have supposedly come to worship! Sprinkle them throughout the auditorium and, before you know it, they have severely dampened whatever enthusiasm for worship may have resided within the true devotees of Christ in the first place. Naturally, getting a larger proportion of worshipers to have a legitimate and significant relationship with Christ will facilitate a more worshipful atmosphere.

At the risk of offending some people, our research also shows that people attending churches associated with certain denominations are more likely to report consistently experiencing God's presence than is true among people attending other types of churches. Importantly, the churches where experiencing true worship is most likely are those affiliated with denominations that have the highest proportion of attenders who are born-again Christians. In contrast, the churches that are least likely to have people who say they have experienced God's presence are those attending churches affiliated with denominations that have the fewest born-again individuals. Although research does not allow us to guarantee that there is a cause and effect relationship between these two factors, the strength of the statistical correlation and the logic underlying this possible connection are worth noting.

COMMITMENT TO WORSHIP

One challenge for churches is to simply get worship on the agenda of attenders. In many congregations worship is just one more activity among a slate of dozens and dozens of options from which to choose. Among the highly effective churches, establishing worship as one of the non-negotiable endeavors of a Christian is a core habit.

In addition to getting people to commit to worship because they recognize how important it is to God and because of their personal gratitude to God for all He has done for them, highly effective churches have made significant gains by challenging people to expect to encounter God. Perhaps this does not sound like a big contribution to the effort to get people to worship. At the first few churches where I encountered this tactic, I dismissed it as an interesting quirk but irrelevant. I was wrong. This is a very important piece to the puzzle.

What happens if a person comes to church hoping to encounter God but not really expecting to make such a connection?

After trying for a while, if a connection is not made, the person gives up. But what happens if the person comes to church not only hoping to make a divine connection but also completely expectant of such interaction? The chances are good that the individual will not give up until the connection is made. Given that God wants to connect with us and that we want to connect with Him, we will persevere much longer in our effort to experience Him than if such a connection is just a pipe dream.

In fact, when people expect God to connect with them, they behave very differently. There is more passion, more energy and more joy invested in worship. People lose some of their culture-based inhibitions about interacting with God in public when they feel assured that He will meet them in a very real way. The other side of the coin is equally true: If people do not expect God to be present, either because of past experience or a general disbelief in interpersonal connection, then the worship that transpires is usually tepid. People are lethargic in their singing, distracted in their prayers, halfhearted in their attentiveness to God's Word. *Expectations make a world of difference in the quality of worship!*

One other element that emerged in studying how effective churches raise the level of commitment to worship relates to people's idea of how much worship is enough. Effective churches teach their people that you can never give God too much worship; He revels in it. Worship is not meant to be simply a Sunday morning activity—it is not something you turn on at 11:00 A.M. on Sunday and switch off at noon, not to be worried about for the next 167 hours. *Worship is meant to be a regular part of our daily existence.* The difference between the Sunday morning worship and our times of personal worship is that Sunday provides a corporate experience. It is different from personal worship, but each form of worship complements and completes the other.

Worship Services That Work

Some church analysts have questioned whether it is even possible to have an effective corporate worship experience in our culture these days. It is a good question to ask, but I believe the answer is an unqualified "Yes, it is possible." However, the nature of worship services must be examined carefully if we hope to offer a truly worshipful experience to those who attend.

One lesson that I learned from the highly effective churches is that worship seems to be most transformational when we intentionally provide worshipers with contrasts embedded within the worship event. Because people have short attention spans these days, they resist routine activity and it takes greater and greater stimulation to keep people involved in their activity. Providing a service that introduces intentional contrasts keeps people interested and involved. Here are examples of some of the contrasts that these ministries intentionally use to engage people in worship:

- the head (preaching) versus the heart (music, prayer);
- order (the service agenda) versus spontaneity (sensitivity to the Holy Spirit);
- reverence (awe of God) versus intimacy (meditation, confession);
- transcendence (supernatural experience) versus accessibility (tangibility, insight);
- security (familiar routines) versus risk (trying new things);
- joy (gratitude) versus contrition (humility);
- expression (singing) versus attentiveness (listening to sermon).

Through the use of such contrasts, people stay more focused and alert, enhancing their ability to remain engaged in the worship experience. Balancing these matters—comfort and discomfort, the old and the new, the easy and the difficult—is more art than science. But, then, so is worship.

WORSHIP MUSIC

During the course of a worship service, most churches use music. Styles vary widely: congregations singing traditional hymns while the pipe organ plays, gospel choirs with piano accompaniment, a band with drums, keyboards, and electric guitars leading contemporary praise and worship choruses, jazz ensembles playing updated versions of classic hymns, solo vocalists backed by a full orchestra, a lone individual strumming an acoustic guitar while leading the congregation in song, etc. Things have changed a lot since the 1950s, when variety in worship music was unusual. Today such variety is critical to worship because music has become such a vital part of personal expression and vocabulary. For the Buster generation, in particular, you could argue that music has become their dominant language.

The role of music in Christian worship is central. But there are numerous issues regarding the use of music in worship—and the response to those issues can be very controversial. Our research enables me to address three important questions of worship/music debate: How much music should there be, what style of music should be used, and who should lead the music in worship?

How much music facilitates genuine worship? As you might have guessed, there is not a "magic number" of minutes that represents the best answer to this query. It seems that there are four factors that work together to determine how much music is included in a worship service. There should be enough to:

- focus people's attention on God and on the act of worship;
- calm people down and soften their hearts toward God;
- facilitate intimacy with God;
- stir their souls.

How long this takes varies from congregation to congregation and may vary from week to week within the same congregation. But here is a rule of thumb that may be helpful: Highly effective churches typically incorporate at least 20 minutes of uninterrupted worship music into their services.

There are two important factors to emphasize in this regard. First, notice that this refers to uninterrupted music. There seems to be significant value to allowing people to find a means of expression to God without having that flow disturbed by other forms of activity or observation. Second, 20 minutes is not a minimum or a maximum ideal in time. It is an average. In fact, the way that many highly effective churches determine how much worship music is enough is based not on the clock but on the congregation. In those churches the worship leader is responsible for "reading the congregation"—that is, evaluating how integrated into worship they are (based on overt signs such as facial language, body language and breadth of participation in the singing). At an appropriate time the leader then transitions from the music to the next part of the worship experience.

I have alluded to the "worship leader." This is a popular but unfortunate term that has been adopted by many churches. It implies that anything that takes place during the service, other than music, is not part of the worship. The term "music leader" seems more appropriate. Whatever the name you prefer, my research emphasized the crucial role played by this person (who, for the sake of convention, we will henceforth call the music leader). He/she is often a paid employee of the church, although in an increasing percentage of churches the music leader is a lay person skilled in the areas of music and worship direction. The key is that the music leader be someone whose presence in front of the congregation during the service fulfills three objectives:

- the music leader gives suitable guidance to the musical expression carried out by the congregation. This is done through various means: verbal cues, hand gestures, call and response, etc.;
- the music leader serves as a model for people to follow or learn from while worshiping in front of the congregation. In some ways the music leader is a coach, someone who mentors people in worship through song while the process is in effect;
- the music leader should direct people's attention to God, removing the spotlight from him or herself and the musicians who may be accompanying, etc.

Great music leaders seem to have a number of qualities in common. Those characteristics include the following:

Great Music Leader Qualities

1. Is completely sold out to Jesus Christ; their faith commitment is intense, deep and central to who they are personally and professionally;
2. Exhibits Christian character: humility, servanthood, repentance, serenity, love, loyalty, kindness, etc.;
3. Remains an active, growing student of Scripture;
4. Is devoted to prayer;

5. Has the gift of leadership which is currently being carried out through music and worship;
6. Is a knowledgeable and skilled musician—although not necessarily a "world class" composer, arranger or performer, since his/her major contribution is in leadership and worship;
7. Reflects a true passion for worship and an obvious ability to worship with integrity and intensity;
8. Is willing to follow the guidance of the Holy Spirit in the worship context, resulting in flexibility (rather than rigidity) during a worship event;
9. Shows unusual sensitivity to the worshipful state of the congregation in the midst of the worship service;
10. Demonstrates responsible submission to the other leaders of the church;
11. Continually grows spiritually;
12. Demonstrates a genuine call to minister through leading worship and a willingness to be authentic, vulnerable and transparent in the worship process.

When you identify such a music leader, turn them loose; the results radically change the personality of the church and the impact of its ministry. They are often very different kinds of people: quiet, reflective and compassionate, yet self-assured and resilient. You will find them to be in love with the Bible and anxious to get others to love God as deeply and as regularly as they do.

Does this discussion of music leaders mean a pastor should not lead the music portion of the worship service? Not necessarily, although only a handful of the highly effective churches examined had a leader/pastor who also led the worship music. Clearly there are some pastors whom God has gifted to facilitate this aspect of the worship event. In most cases, though, it seems that the pastor's true calling lies elsewhere and the congregation might be better served by the pastor serving in those other dimensions of the ministry.

One of the most contested questions concerns the appropriate styles of music for worship. The research findings suggest that having worship music that engages people's hearts through participation best facilitates worship. To do so the *music should be accessible to the average person* in terms of the keys used, how many stanzas are sung, the currency of the language in the lyrics, the simplicity of the melodies, etc. Remember that most Americans have little musical knowledge; even reading the musical notation in a hymnal is beyond the capacity of the average adult. To escalate people's involvement in singing songs of worship to God—and truly getting something out of it—simplify the process.

BLENDED WORSHIP

Recent years have raised the issue of "blended worship" which usually means incorporating two or more styles of music into the service. Our research shows that such worship can be very effective—but only within certain parameters. It may be worth noting, by the way, that most of the highly effective churches use a single musical style in a service—few of them engage in "blended worship."

The blended approach seems to work best when four conditions are met. First, each style of music should be related to the content of the service or flow from a philosophy of ministry that emphasizes the character and special meaning of different musical styles. Second, the congregation must have been adequately prepared for the different styles used and have the ability to appreciate why and how each style of music meets the worship objective of the service. Third, the lyrics of each song must have depth and meaning, regardless of the style. Finally, blended worship is most effective when no more than two different styles of music are used in the same service. Although a church can effectively use many different styles over the course of time, more than two styles in a single service can become distracting or confusing for people. It does appear that concentrating on just two or three styles that are used consistently maximizes the congregation's ability to appreciate those musical formats.

There are also some conditions under which multiple musical styles do not facilitate worship. The most common problem is when the divergent styles are used primarily as a marketing device. In thousands of churches two or three different approaches are used in a service for the purpose of giving different segments of the congregation something they can each enjoy. The problem is that rather than drawing each audience segment into a deeper worship experience, this strategy more often generates frustration over having to sit through several different styles that cannot be justified for inclusion on the basis of a worship-related reason.

People do not attend church for music education; they know what they like and what they will tolerate and are easily annoyed if they feel they are being manipulated. This concern is especially acute among Busters and Boomers. For both of these groups, music is almost sacred; they crave musical expression but possess very low levels of tolerance for music that they cannot comprehend or that seems antiquated. Other potential problems concerning blended worship include the use of music the people do not understand or music that does not connect to the content of their worship, the use of too many styles, and the use of songs or styles of music that do not flow well with each other.

PREACHING AND TEACHING AS WORSHIP

The focal point of most worship services is the sermon. We have discovered that the sermon is the only exposure to Christian teaching that most church-going adults in America have in a typical week. Clearly, the sermon remains an important element in the faith development process. But once again it became evident that many highly effective churches have pioneered ways of maximizing the impact of the sermon—even in a country and during an era when people don't like to be told what to do, especially in a Bible-based, lecture format.

The first lesson from the highly effective churches is that people have to be taught how to hear truth. The first step in that process is often challenging people's views of Scripture. The highly effective churches invariably taught that the Bible is a source of truth and can be relied upon to provide wisdom for all dimensions of life. Once people embrace this notion, it removes many of the doubts and intellectual conflicts that prevent them from grappling with the implications and applications of biblical content.

The second factor that enhances the influence of preaching is consistently motivating people to spend time in earnest, private confession of their sins. This is a cleansing process that prepares people to connect with God through His Word. It is amazing how many churches have no time during their worship event for private confession, nor a regular process through which people are encouraged to seek God's forgiveness for their sins. The pastors of the effective churches confided that while they have no hard evidence to support their contention, they believe that this is one of the secrets to preaching that changes lives. Because the people have humbled themselves before God through their act of self-examination and confession, they are open to absorbing God's exhortations to them.

Third, highly effective pastors also attribute the impact of their preaching to the conscious shaping of congregants' expectations. One pastor called this his "heart massage" process. In

Every one of the

preachers from the highly

effective churches

concurred that preaching

has impact only if the

audience perceives

practical value in

the sermon.

essence, the preacher informs people, through stories and direct admonitions, that Christianity (as understood through his/her preaching) is not designed to make people comfortable, happy or flattered. The teaching of Jesus produced pain, discomfort, insecurity and hardships. When combined with a perspective that the Bible is a source of truth and with serious exhortations to engage God through confession, these three tactics equip people to hear and to handle God's truth as communicated by the preacher.

Every one of the preachers from the highly effective churches concurred that preaching has impact only if the audience perceives practical value in the sermon. Among the keys to providing such value were the provision of credible applications, reliance upon stories and realistic illustrations to convey a point, and a preaching style that portrayed the preacher as open, honest, accessible and empathetic. Our quantitative study of preaching concluded that preaching style is often more memorable than sermon substance, even among the best of preachers. Adults are more than twice as likely to remember the way a preacher delivered the sermon as they are to recall the major theological points, the stories or the personal applications. The words flowing from a preacher's mouth are often the least important message being communicated.

Our national study on preaching revealed several other insights that may help preachers to be more effective. We know that pastors work hard at preparing their sermons; in fact, they usually spend more time on sermon preparation than on any other activity they undertake during a typical week. However, pastors often make some unwarranted assumptions about the capacity of the audience. Briefly, here are some discoveries regarding those assumptions:

- The language used by pastors is often more sophisticated than the congregation can understand. Our content analysis of sermons indicates that the typical sermon requires a 12th grade literacy level, yet the average church-goer has about an 8th grade literacy level.
- The average sermon in Protestant churches today lasts 32 minutes. With the attention span of Americans constantly diminishing—our studies among Baby Busters, for instance, estimate their attention span in the 6- to 10-minute range—most sermons suffer from a "phasing" problem. People phase in and out of the sermon, catching some parts and missing others, rendering these well-constructed arguments less effective than most preachers hope for. Techniques for enhancing content retention—intermittent visual aids, vocal pitch variation, staggered presentations and even shorter sermons—have been shown to heighten recall and impact.

- Some preachers are doomed from the start because they have not developed sufficient credibility in the minds of listeners. In this age of skepticism, establishing credibility is a precursor to pedagogical impact. This may be achieved through relational intimacy with congregants, a lifestyle that is consistent with one's exhortations and a track record of providing pragmatic and theologically trustworthy messages.

A WORSHIP FRIENDLY ENVIRONMENT

Another critical worship dimension addressed by highly effective churches is the environment within which worship occurs. Based on widespread observations I would argue that it is possible to have good preaching and good music in a service, but still have a vapid worship experience. Often, such a flat event can be attributed to the worship setting.

Highly effective churches deserve credit for highlighting the importance of prayer in worship. They incorporate prayer in four key ways. First, they have teams of praying congregants seeking God's provision for the worship experience both before the service begins as well as during the service. Second, the preachers at these churches spend a substantial amount of time during the week praying that their message will hit home with everyone. Some of the preachers at these churches spend equal amounts of time in prayer and in sermon preparation—and the former undeniably strengthens the latter. Third, during the worship service there are times set aside for prayer—not the dry, rote, mindless prayer of some churches, but a heartfelt, serious conversation with God that is related to the content or focus of the service. Fourth, these churches have staff, lay leaders and prayer teams that cumulatively spend hours and hours during the week praying for the forthcoming service. They do this every week, without fail. The pastors interviewed all had tales of woe regarding the weeks when such prayer was neglected. Prayer matters, and these churches make the most of its power.

One of the more unique aspects of worship services at highly effective churches is that one never knows exactly how long they will last. This is not for lack of planning or due to unprofessionalism; it is because of sensitivity to the Holy Spirit. Despite an order of service that has been developed with great care during the week—and is sometimes preceded by rehearsals that further refine the timing of the service—there is sufficient flexibility in these services to allow for a change of plans prompted by the Spirit. One leader/pastor described this as his determination to "give God room to move; I don't want to be guilty of insisting on my human agenda instead of His perfect agenda." So how long are the services at highly effective churches? Long enough to allow people to truly connect with God, but short enough to maximize people's focus on God and maintain the quality of the experience. They know that a service that runs too long can dissipate the impact while a service that is curtailed too early may preclude people from achieving a peak worship experience.

Ministering with such flexibility is often a struggle for leader/pastors. One of them, a Southern Baptist leader/pastor, spoke of his discomfort with the indeterminate length of his church's services.

My seminary professor taught us how to time services down to the half-minute. While still in school I interned for a pastor who set a time for the service and was never off by more than 60 seconds, the whole time I served there. Then I took an associate position at a church and worked with a senior [pastor] who ran the service like a military operation. Again, there was no slack. I was trained to figure out what you're gonna do and then you do it, just as you planned. Any interference was not God's way of doing things.

So naturally I came here and my tendency was to agonize over every minute of the service and have very tight control on timing. But then the Holy Spirit started working in me and, before you know it, I was convinced and then I persuaded the staff and elders that we needed to be open to the Holy Spirit visiting us in some unusual ways. None of us, myself included, were at all comfortable with this in the beginning. And you know us, we're pretty by the book, but once we made the shift [to greater flexibility] some very powerful things have happened.

One Sunday I was totally convinced that the Holy Spirit was calling upon me not to preach my sermon. Now is that blasphemy to a Baptist preacher or what? But instead the Spirit was pushing me to lead us in a concert of prayer. I wish you could have seen me up there. It must have looked like I was schizophrenic, wrestling with my two minds that morning. [Here he imitated the two voices that were struggling inside of him.] "I have to preach"; "I can't preach." "God wouldn't want His people to go home without exposure to His Word"; "His people don't need that today, they need something else." "This church counts on me to provide a strong message every week"; "this church hired you to lead them in ways that honor God"; and so on. I tell you what, we did that morning of prayer and people were just being blessed left and right. At the end of the morning we had an altar call, which was really odd because three-quarters of 'em was already kneeling in the aisles or on the platform steps, and we had more commitments that morning than at any other service that year. Our services usually run about 75 minutes, but that one ran close to two hours.

I'm telling you, there were some miracles that morning—and none of them would have happened if I'd stuck to the plan and I'd preached my message. I am a firm—and I mean firm—believer in staying tuned into the Holy Spirit, even if it's not popular among a lot of my colleagues. I've seen what God can do when you're on His page instead of your own. But it really does take a lot of courage and getting used to.

The power of continuity is another lesson that effective churches have learned. But again, continuity means more than just a seamless mixture of worship components. The significant lesson absorbed by so many of these churches was, again, countercultural: Simplicity in worship is more valuable than having a slick, over-produced event. Thus, at the very time when churches across the land are striving to achieve greater production values—full orchestras or bands, theatrical presentations, video-projection systems, professional sound and lighting—the highly effective churches stand out for the ability to implement such elements, but their determination is to forego many of the bells and whistles and instead go simple. Why? "This is worship. The more complex or riveting we make the process, the less people focus on God," was the simple explanation of one leader/pastor. Rather than the usual seven or eight elements a typical service might incorporate, numerous highly effective churches have reduced their services to just three or four elements—raw, simple, unvarnished, but genuine, professional and sincere.

I also had a deep appreciation for the effective church's emphasis upon strategic attention to environmental details. Two common threads stood out. First, they tend to the "staging" elements of the service—sound, lighting, temperature control, lines of visual contact—to ensure a smooth service and a glitch-free sanctuary. Their objective is to guarantee that worshipers are not distracted by anything—a burned-out light bulb, a buzzing sound system, uncomfortably warm temperatures, an obstructed view of the platform, etc. The leader/pastor of a midsized church in the Northeast explained: "My goal is to remove any physical failing that could possibly take their attention away from God. Satan will use anything to break our union with God, and I will do anything I can to ensure that those potential temptations to disengage from worship are eliminated."

Highly effective churches have also thought through how to handle other distractions. They have planned responses for things such as the seating of latecomers (solution: never seat them in highly visible sections of the church), children who cry during the service (solution: special "cry rooms" or sound-proofed seating areas with closed-circuit video for parents with cranky kids), the distribution of programs with announcements (solution: hand out an order of service upon entering, distribute the announcements on a separate page upon exiting), etc. These churches have identified the conditions that promote worship and those that prevent worship; they have responded purposefully to both.

INTENTIONAL EVALUATION

For churches, facilitating great worship means that you leave as little to chance as possible. Highly effective churches accomplish this by regularly, honestly and comprehensively evaluating everything that happens in relation to worship. They identify people who can provide honest and valuable feedback about the worship services. They develop a refined list of measurable criteria through which the services can be consistently assessed. They maintain a firm commitment to making necessary changes when shortcomings are identified or when superior ideas are conceived. These churches are a living testimony to the reality that improvement only comes through commitment to honest self-evaluation.

In the end, highly effective churches excel in worship because they take a no-holds-barred approach to connecting people to God. A church that does not consistently and whole-heartedly worship God is a spiritually anemic church. Highly effective churches have discovered the antidote to spiritual anemia: genuine, dynamic churchwide worship!

NOTE
1. In our surveys we ask two questions the answers to which are used to characterize a person as a Christian. The first question is "Have you ever made a personal commitment to Jesus Christ that is still important in your life today?" If respondents answer "yes," they are asked the second question in which they must choose one of seven alternatives about what they believe will happen to them after they die on earth. One of the options is "When I die I will go to heaven because I have confessed my sins and have accepted Jesus Christ as my savior." People who answer these questions in this manner are then labeled "born-again Christians" or simply "Christians," regardless of how they describe themselves spiritually.

ENGAGING IN STRATEGIC EVANGELISM

More than four out of five Protestant pastors describe their churches as "evangelistic." What separates the highly effective churches from the rest when it comes to evangelism is not that they believe more intensely in evangelism or that they preach more often on the significance of sharing the Christian faith with non-Christians. They stand out because they engage in *evangelism in a strategic manner.*

It is not uncommon for a Protestant church to uphold the importance of evangelism yet see only a handful of converts, if any, resulting from the evangelistic efforts of its church members.

This is at least partially due to the random nature of the church's approach to evangelism. In contrast, highly effective churches treat evangelism like every other task they face: It must be studied, the action options must be analyzed and compared, direction from God must be earnestly sought, choices must be made, people must be informed and prepared, and then the plans must be put into practice.

This systematic approach seems too routine to some pastors, but the highly effective churches maintain passion and excitement for the privilege of evangelizing and for the prospect of success throughout the process. And they are classy in how they approach evangelism: Their passion to be agents of transformation is balanced with a respect for the people whom they wish to reach, the believers whom they are counting on to reach them and the power of God to fulfill His promises.

Eliminating Negative Pressure on Evangelism

Christians who attend highly effective churches share their faith consistently with nonbelievers. Not everyone in these congregations does so, of course, but these ministries have a larger proportion of evangelizers than is the norm among churches. I believe this is largely because highly effective churches intentionally eliminate a lot of the negative pressure that surrounds the act of evangelism in our society.

Negative pressure regarding evangelism is placed on Christians in many different ways. Some churches do so by establishing unrealistic expectations ("everyone in this congregation should be winning at least one person to Christ every month"). Some congregations, perhaps unintentionally, seek to motivate evangelism through guilt ("if you're not a soul winner, you're letting Jesus down," "God's kingdom depends upon you to actively and unashamedly tell everyone you know about salvation through Christ"). I have even visited some churches that turned evangelism into a competitive sport ("we will celebrate the person who leads the most people to Christ at our 'Penetrating the Darkness' banquet next week").

Highly effective churches, however, recognize that even though every believer has a responsibility to tell others about Christ, we all have different gifts and abilities. These churches therefore do not disparage people whose evangelistic ventures are few and far between or who may seem less successful than might be desired. In fact, the key to understanding evangelism in highly effective churches is to realize that they define success in evangelism as intelligently taking advantage of every reasonable opportunity to evangelize that God provides to them. For various reasons some people will have fewer evangelistic opportunities than might be available to other believers. If a person is honestly seeking to be obedient to the leading of the Holy Spirit in faith encounters, then a highly effective church will applaud his/her willingness to do God's will in God's timing, regardless of the outcome.

To some this may seem a bit brazen or callous. After all, isn't the local church supposed to enhance the efforts of its evangelizers and shouldn't it be zealous to win everyone to Christ as quickly as possible? My observations of highly effective churches found that they are truly passionate about evangelism and make no excuses about the importance of exploiting every evangelistic opportunity that is available. However, a crucial perspective moderates their zeal: Humans do not convert nonbelievers; only the Holy Spirit can do that. Consequently, our responsibility is to serve as capable conduits of God's love through a clear expression of the gospel message. Whether or not the person accepts Christ is beyond human control. The quality of our evangelistic efforts does matter, the leaders of these churches contend, but there are limits as to how much one ought to agonize over the outcome of an evangelistic encounter.

To maximize the probability of a nonbeliever accepting Christ, highly effective churches teach that the foundation of viable evangelism is relationships. These churches encourage people to be *intentionally networked to nonbelievers* and to build up true friendships with those people so that when a good opportunity to share Christ occurs they have the *credibility* and *trust* in place to support their presentation of the gospel.

To facilitate the networking and the evangelistic efforts of congregants, highly effective churches do everything they can to support their people. First, they provide low-key, seeker-friendly events that congregants can unashamedly attend with their non-Christian friends. Some churches have a weekly "seeker service" designed to introduce nonbelievers to Christianity; others sponsor special events ranging from "Friends Day" to pre-evangelistic softball games or family outings. Second, these churches provide evangelistic training for all who are interested in being more effective in sharing their faith. Third, these churches make resources available to the congregation regarding evangelism. Those resources range from books and tapes about evangelism to special seminars on witnessing or apologetics.

Perhaps the secret to removing unnecessary pressure in evangelism, though, is in positioning evangelism positively. Highly effective churches portray evangelism as an act of love for other people, rather than as a means of proving one's self-worth through productive witnessing. When evangelism is a matter of obligation, it then becomes a performance whose quality determines one's personal value. When sharing our faith in Christ becomes a matter of the heart, however, our motivations are pure and both our strategies and persistence are more likely to produce positive outcomes. I believe this explains why the highly effective churches have a much higher rate of numerical growth from conversions than from transfers of believers from other churches.

MATCHING PEOPLE AND PROCESS

It is no secret that most Christians avoid evangelism. Despite this, highly effective churches usually have a majority of their people actively sharing their faith with nonbelievers. This is not because they attract people who are gifted as evangelists. Besides eliminating negative pressure to evangelize, highly effective churches increase the odds of successful evangelism by helping believers match their evangelistic style to the nature of the person they are seeking to influence.

A couple of years ago we conducted an enlightening study regarding evangelistic tactics. The conclusion that emerged was simple but very significant: Different people groups respond to different evangelistic approaches. For instance, young adults responded best to what I called "Socratic evangelism"—an approach in which a Christian engages a nonbeliever in a conversation about a nonreligious issue that is important to the non-Christian. During the course of the conversation, the Christian never tells the non-Christian that he/she is dumb for not accepting Christ, or that Jesus is the answer to all issues in life, or that there is only one means to truth. Instead, the Christian listens carefully to what the non-Christian has to say about the issue under consideration and inquires as to why the nonbeliever holds such opinions—not in a threatening or offensive way, but in a manner which thoughtfully prods the nonbeliever to clarify his/her stance.

Eventually, all issues do come down to a spiritual perspective. Over the course of several interactions, in which the conversation on that issue gets deeper and deeper, it will invariably reach a spiritual level—and a spiritual conclusion. Through this approach *a skilled Socratic evangelist can lead a person to Christ in a very natural way.* Individuals who accept Christ in response to a Socratic process tend to be more zealously committed to Christ and to changing their lives because they were not manipulated into accepting a particular viewpoint. The Socratic method allows them to draw any conclusion, but more often than not they conclude of their own volition that Christ is the divine Savior of humankind and must be personally embraced.[1]

Evangelism Effectiveness Rating Scale, by Generation

●●●● major harvesting   ●●● good choice   ●● so-so
● bad stewardship   shame on you

evangelism method	Busters	Boomers	Builders	Seniors
lifestyle/friendship	●●●	●●●	●●●	●●●
family	●●	●●	●●	●
confrontational		●	●●	●
cell group	●●●	●●	●	●
power evangelism	●●●	●●●	●●	●●
mass media		●	●●	●●
mass crusades	●●	●●	●	
affinity group meetings	●●	●●●	●●	●
social welfare outreach	●●●●	●●	●●	●
youth rallies	●●			
concerts	●●●	●●	●	●
drama	●●	●●	●	
sports participation	●●	●●	●	
church planting	●	●●	●	
traditional church services	●	●	●●	●●
contemporary seeker services	●●	●●●	●	
Sunday school class	●	●●	●●●	●●
church sponsored events	●●	●●	●	●●
Socratic evangelism	●●●●	●●	●	●
literature outreach		●	●●	●●●

Source: Barna Research Group, Ltd., 1998

Figure 5.1

Effective churches are able to help congregants understand the different types of non-Christians they will encounter and how to "read" them for evangelistic purposes. The purpose of doing so is not to manipulate them into God's kingdom but to do just the opposite: to provide nonbelievers with information or an experience that accepts who they are and recognizes what they need to make an informed decision about Christ.

The philosophy behind this approach is that there is not just one appropriate way to share the gospel with nonbelievers. However, Christians must be prepared to understand different methods of sharing their faith with non-Christians, based upon an accurate understanding of what approaches would speak most clearly to the needs and perceptual abilities of the non-believer.

COUNTING ON KIDS

Highly effective churches are strategic in their evangelistic efforts in another way, too: They devote most of their evangelistic resources to reaching kids. Our research shows that a majority of people who accept Christ as their Savior do so before the age of 18—nearly two out of three believers. In fact, a majority makes that crucial decision between the ages of 8 and 14. Thus, focusing on young people is a wise investment of the church's limited evangelistic resources.

In the highly effective churches there is an effort to reach people of all ages; an emphasis upon young people does not mean that the salvation of older people is ignored. However, these churches want to maximize their influence for Christ and therefore make the most of the apparent opportunity. Across the board these churches note that evangelism among adolescents and early teens is also a much simpler process than is trying to penetrate the hardened defenses of adults.

One of the implications of this reality, by the way, is that the youth pastor is not merely a caretaker or Bible teacher but is the church's primary evangelist. Think about that when you search for your next youth pastor!

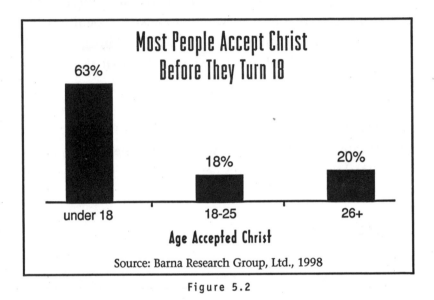

Most People Accept Christ Before They Turn 18

63% — under 18
18% — 18-25
20% — 26+

Age Accepted Christ

Source: Barna Research Group, Ltd., 1998

Figure 5.2

CONVERSIONS, NOT DECISIONS

Perhaps the most essential element behind the evangelistic success of these churches is their insistence that evangelism be inextricably married to discipleship. Conversion to Christianity is not just seen as merely a decision, but the goal of evangelistic efforts is to see new believers grow in Christ.

The distinction between conversions and decisions might sound like simple semantics, but our extensive research on this matter shows that it is much deeper than a difference of terminology. What happens is that many churches present the good news about salvation through grace in a service or public event and ask non-Christian people to make a decision to follow Christ. The church then essentially abandons the individuals who make such a decision; they may be prayed with, given a Bible and other literature and encouraged to join in the classes and programs of the church, but then they are left alone while the church focuses on reaching other non-Christians. In recent studies, we discovered that a majority of people who made a decision for Christ were no longer connected to a Christian church within a short period—usually 8 to 12 weeks—after their initial decision.

I don't want to be unduly harsh toward these churches; their intentions are honorable and they commit themselves to doing evangelism in a way they believe is likely to be effective. The problem is one of misunderstanding. These churches misunderstand the person they seek to evangelize; they assume that the individual knows much more about Christianity and spiritual development than is the case. They also assume that because the decision the person is making is so important, the new Christian will doggedly pursue spiritual growth. At the same time, the person making the decision misunderstands the very nature of the decision being made. Few of them have a deep enough comprehension of the implications of the decision they are making to foster a strategic commitment to Christianity and the development of their personal faith.

The other aspect of the misunderstanding relates to the persons making the decision for Christ. We discovered that many of these people thought they were agreeing to explore the Christian faith more deeply. Many of them heard the language used to describe salvation by grace—"having a relationship with Jesus," "turning their lives over to Christ," "being saved from eternal damnation by the debt paid on their behalf at Calvary," "accepting God's grace for eternity"—but did not grasp the practical meaning of these phrases. Many of them had no inkling that there was more to real Christianity than raising their hand or fill-

Highly effective churches

maintain you cannot

separate evangelism

from discipleship.

ing out a decision card or kneeling at an altar and repeating "the sinner's prayer." Consequently, after the decision was made and the literature passed along, they assumed they had done all that was required to get their "free gift" (i.e., eternal life) and now they could move on with life.

Most of these people are left alone by their church after having made their "commitment," which reinforces their natural assumption that they must have done whatever it is a person does to become a Christian and life then goes on as "business as usual." Many of them, eternal fire insurance now acquired, depart from the church to pursue other interests. The failure of the evangelizing body to follow up adequately leaves numerous people spiritually crippled; they think they are truly Christian and have gone as far as a person needs to go spiritually when, in fact, they have barely begun the Christian journey.

Highly effective churches maintain that if you are going to engage in evangelism at all, you have an obligation to finish the job. That means not only telling people the good news of Christ's atoning death on the cross and subsequent resurrection, but ensuring that through a personalized spiritual growth process people who make a "decision" to embrace Jesus also become converted to following Him with all their heart, mind, soul and strength. These churches assert that you cannot separate evangelism from discipleship; the former without the latter is simply religious marketing, and the latter without the former builds on a foundation of sand.

The evangelistic efforts of highly effective churches are therefore very relational. They do not conduct evangelistic events unless those events are based on pre-existing relationships, which then allow the Christian who has befriended the spiritually seeking nonbeliever to follow up any residual questions or decisions in an environment of trust and understanding.

These churches recognize that we do not have the ability to convert a person; only the Holy Spirit can transform an individual. Their people see themselves as conduits in the evangelistic process. Highly effective churches do their best to create situations and relationships through which informed and equipped believers can intelligently and diligently participate in the conversion process.

THE ROLE OF MISSIONS

In recent years Americans have shown greater interest in investing in local or national needs than in sending money and people overseas to assist those in need in other nations. This has caused somewhat of a panic among global missions agencies. It has become more difficult not only to attract missionaries to send into the field, but also more difficult to raise the money required to fund such missionary efforts.

Highly effective churches often attract people who prefer funding local ministry efforts to global activities, but those views are challenged through the teaching and activities of the church. One of the objectives of most highly effective churches is to sustain a healthy balance between local and global missions. Local missions activity serves several critical purposes: helping people in need, providing believers with a tangible way of enacting their faith, uniting the congregation through acts of service, focusing believers on the needs of others, etc. But a core value of local outreach is that it paves the way for discussions and strategies pertaining to international missions. The church challenges its people not to choose between supporting either local or global ministry, but to address needs at both levels.

PARTICIPATORY MISSIONS

Interestingly, the way in which many highly effective churches accomplish this objective is by encouraging participatory global missions activity. While most churches are content to send money to missionaries or missions agencies, highly effective churches disdain such a "soft" commitment. One pastor called that approach "buying off your obligation—no emotional investment, just a financial write-off." Given the ministry philosophy of effective churches (ministry is about *personal investment in people's lives,* not about funding professional ministers to do ministry in their stead), facilitating a personal interest in missions is paramount.

This is accomplished by getting the congregation to carefully investigate missions options and make personal choices and commitments regarding international missions opportunities. In a typical highly effective church, here is the process:

First, the pastor and key leaders teach about the necessity of involvement in worldwide missions—local, national and global. The leaders set parameters for the church's missions giving—usually stated as a minimum financial goal based upon past missions giving and current budgets. The church does not, however, dictate where the missions money will go.

Next, individuals who are most enthusiastic about some of the missions opportunities that exist organize a discovery team. Their purpose is to do the homework that leads to a decision to support or ignore a specific missions opportunity. This team gets second-hand information (such as reports and plans) from a ministry that is under consideration for support. If the ministry meets the established criteria in the first pass of investigation, then the team typically sends one or more representatives to the place of ministry for on-site examination. Upon returning, the traveling investigators make their report—usually complete with photographs and videotaped highlights of the trip— and the team then issues its "go/no go" recommendation to the church. At that point, it is up to the members of the group or entire church—depending upon who has the funding authority—to accept or reject the discovery team's recommendation. That recommendation is rarely turned down.

Perhaps this sounds unrealistic, expensive, too labor intensive, overly democratic or excessively time consuming. These are common misgivings voiced by churches that operate in a more traditional, hierarchical decision-making style. Consider, however, some of the major benefits received from the participatory approach:

- *Provides Personal Involvement for Everyone*
  Missions come alive for many people because they have the freedom and authority to make the decisions about what types of ministry they want to support. This is no longer an inherited obligation but a self-determined extension of personal ministry.

• *Creates Responsible Stewardship*

Nobody is forcing the church to support an overseas denominational ministry or an organization that has been supported by the church because of the political maneuvering of one or a few church insiders. The discovery process increases the sense of accountability for the decision to support—and to maintain ongoing support for—a global ministry venture.

• *Awakens Distinct Involvement in Certain People*

Believers who ordinarily might not have a role in ministry sometimes become intensely involved in ministry through this hands-on, research-oriented evaluation process.

• *Creates a Deeper Emotional Investment*

Effective churches are unusual in that they receive regular reports about their supported global works from their missions-minded members—and the rest of the congregation appreciates (rather than endures) such reports because a sense of ownership has been nurtured on these projects.

• *Creates Awareness that Missions is a Worldwide Endeavor*

"One Faith, one Church" was the expression used by one of the highly effective churches to characterize its renewed understanding of how its small body of believers was able to reach distant parts of the world through intentional and informed ministry investing and spiritual connections.

• Encourages Prayer

These churches take prayer for missions seriously. They have teams of people who pray regularly for the missionary colleagues they support. My sense is that the prayer for their missionary partners is not done out of a sense of obligation but from a heart of genuine concern and gratitude for the partners' efforts.

• Allows Laypeople To Become Advocates of Missionary Efforts

The participatory process means that missions activities have avid advocates within the congregation. The pastor or other staff need not assume the role of "the defender of missions." Instead, if a staff person is delegated the role of overseeing missions activity, that primary duty is defined as supporting the work of the lay missions advocates in the church.

• Provides Opportunities for Church Members to Actively Go to the Mission Field

The church's sense of doing ministry is enhanced because its own members are not just praying for others to do ministry—they are doing ministry themselves. This appears to be a very empowering benefit of participatory missions: The people take reasonable pride in the fact that they are "doers of the Word."

What triggers such an unusual commitment to participation in global missions? In most cases it was the leader/pastor identifying individuals who were likely to flourish in such an environment of decentralized decision-making, describing the possibilities to those individuals and turning them loose to make it happen. Again, the value of the previously described habit of a ministry structure that esteems decentralization and delegation becomes evident. When retaining control of the ministry is a standard operating procedure, effective ministry is often thwarted.

NOTE

1. For more information on this particular form of evangelism, see chapter 7 of my book *Evangelism That Works* (Ventura, CA: Regal Books, 1996).

FACILITATING SYSTEMATIC THEOLOGICAL GROWTH

6

The Christian Church seeks to be many things, but among the most important of its functions is to develop people. If life transformation is the essence of the task facing the local church, then theological education is certainly a core element within that challenge. Perhaps that is why I find the deep-rooted ignorance of Christians about their faith to be so disturbing. This problem is pervasive within the community of believers: *Christians don't know the content of their faith and show little concern about their*

ignorance. This lack of spiritual knowledge and wisdom has resulted in a body of believers that is both incapable of applying their faith in daily circumstances and unable to persuasively share their faith with those who so desperately need it. What a contrast to the Bible's constant exhortation to passionately study His Word, to grow in God's knowledge and wisdom and to provide a sound reason to the unbelieving world as to why we follow Christ (see Col. 1:9; 2 Tim. 2:15; 1 Pet. 3:15, 2 Pet. 1:5).

The problem, of course, is not that the Christian faith does not have the answers to life's challenges that people need; the problem is that most Christians do not devote anything but a spare minute here and there to grappling with the underpinnings and personal implications of Christian theology. Most churches seem to have acquiesced to people's determination to paint happy faces on their Bibles and to keep all teaching and related discussions about faith matters at an elementary level. Few Christians engage in serious theological dialogue because they are simply incapable of sustaining a sophisticated conversation about their faith. The superficiality of Christians' faith is evident in their lifestyles and their general absence from discussions of religious thought and life that should naturally occur in the public square.

Perhaps this condition is what makes the approach to faith education at highly effective churches so refreshing. They do not perceive Christian education to be an ancillary option; at these churches theology is serious business. Working hard at comprehending Christian theology and its personal implications is viewed as a necessary component in the development of each believer. These churches are preparing people for spiritual battle and for a personal renaissance that is founded upon a deep, stimulating, consistent and revolutionary faith system.

These churches are not content with simply offering a full

slate of Sunday School classes and a few special presentations or events during the year. More often than not they serve as theological seminaries for the laity, but with a deeper commitment to the practical application of theological principles. Observing the common educational practices of these churches brought to mind three anonymous quotes I have run across over the years:

"Education is knowing what you want, knowing where to get it and knowing what to do with it after you get it."

"The mind is like a stomach. It's not how much you put in that counts, but how much is digested."

"Tell me and I'll forget. Show me and I may remember. Involve me and I'll understand."

These statements accurately capture the spirit of the Christian formation process in highly effective churches. These churches do not undertake Christian education, discipleship and faith development simply because they are traditional activities of a church. Their educational efforts are designed to produce personal spiritual growth that reflects a well-conceived and carefully developed philosophy and practice of Christian maturity.

Our research concludes that fewer than 10 percent of all born-again Christians possess a biblical worldview that informs their thinking and behavior.[1] A Search Institute survey suggests that most church-going adults have a faith that inadequately integrates the vertical and horizontal dimensions of their Christianity.[2] In contrast, highly effective churches intentionally provide systematic theological education to all of their people. Theirs is a model desperately needed by the American Church as an antidote to the spiritual ignorance and biblical illiteracy of our nation's believers. These churches implement a systematic educational approach to address two primary ends: to ensure that each person has a realistic opportunity to become a complete believer (a comprehensively mature Christian), and to facilitate the development and use of a biblical worldview for decision-making.

Three facets of the faith development process of these churches stand out: their philosophy of Christian development, the methods they use to facilitate faith development and the integration of resources into the process. Let's examine each of these three facets more closely.

A Powerful Underlying Philosophy

The Christian formation philosophy of highly effective churches is not an ambiguous belief in the importance of formal Bible-related education. Their philosophy is a clear, precise, painstakingly developed perspective on the goal of the Church and the contours of the "ideal Christian." They are under no illusion that they can create the perfect believer. However, they contend that a strategic developmental process can result in believers who are overtly and undeniably influenced and driven by their faith. Highly effective churches see one of the major values they provide to congregants as being this educational and developmental function.

The core philosophy embraced by these churches is that Bible knowledge and application must completely influence a person's mind and heart in order for spiritual maturity to be achieved. Understanding the content of the Christian faith—and knowing how to apply it to daily circumstances—is viewed as a long-term life priority for every believer. The process should begin at a young age and continue until death; Christian maturity is regarded as a lifelong pursuit—a journey rather than a specific destination that one may reach and then dismiss.

Appropriate faith development activities should influence the total person including all opinions, attitudes, values, character attributes, behaviors and beliefs. This demands a developmental process that is comprehensive, tying together a person's intellectual, physical, emotional and spiritual growth. The ultimate goal is a sophisticated and complete integration of an individual's faith and lifestyle. Instead of compartmentalizing faith as an important but fragmented portion of a person's existence, an effective developmental process weaves a pragmatic spiritual understanding through every fiber of the person's existence. Religious beliefs and practices become as central to the person's being as eating, sleeping and interrelating.

This philosophy advances the notion that Christians should be

Christians should be a

reflective people

where religious

beliefs and practices

become as central

to the person's

being as eating,

sleeping and

interrelating.

a reflective people. Centuries ago this was not an especially noteworthy view; the dominant societal view was that a reflective life was a natural and desirable state of being. In today's culture, however, reflection is typically deemed to be the domain of philosophers, scholars and retired people—that is, individuals who have the luxury of time to think about such esoteric things as the reasons for our actions or the implications of our choices. The rest of us it seems are too overwhelmed by information, financial pressures, leisure options and other demands to devote much energy to reflection.

In order to translate their philosophy of the value of faith reflection and application to reality, highly effective churches prioritize the learning function of the church. This goes well beyond merely exposing people to a well-reasoned, pragmatic sermon every week. These churches provide an integrated and multifaceted menu of developmental alternatives. The lynchpin of the entire process is the Bible—not what renowned scholars have said about the Bible or people's feelings about Scripture, but the actual content of the Bible itself. God's Word is more than "highly esteemed" at such churches; it is the focal point of their developmental endeavors.

THE ROLE OF THE STUDENT

One distinctive within this philosophy is that the central figure is the student, not the teacher. Both have significant roles to play, but rather than focus on the information and communication style of the teacher, the emphasis is upon the needs, the commitment and the success of the student.

For the developmental process to achieve its potential, though, the student must be motivated to diligently pursue complete spiritual maturity—which, by definition, is beyond human grasp. To diffuse the natural tendency to become discouraged or to avoid the developmental process altogether, highly effective churches use several "carrots" to motivate a life-long, intense commitment to the developmental process. Those motivations include the unwavering acceptance of the Bible's admonition for believers to engage in the endless pursuit of spiritual enlightenment and wholeness, the establishment of clear expectations, the identification of measurable goals, the presence of appropriate role models, the celebration of personal growth, and a realistic perspective on the value of spiritual growth.

For any church that accepts the responsibility for fostering spiritual development in its adherents, such a task requires that the church respect each student. In my observations of the highly effective churches, such respect is operationalized in three ways. First, the church respects the student's time. Not only is time the dominant currency in today's society, but Scripture exhorts us to make the most of the time we have at our disposal (see Ps. 90:12; 1 Cor. 7:29-31). Highly effective churches therefore eliminate busy work and unproductive or unpromising exercises in favor of activities that have a proven track record or high potential. In other words, the developmental process majors on the essentials.

Second, highly effective churches establish high standards to which they are held accountable—of their own volition. These churches set high expectations for their students and plan to meet those expectations. The failure to achieve the goals that have been so thoughtfully determined triggers a rigorous examination of the developmental process. If the student has truly invested himself/herself in the faith development process, the church is committed to ensuring that the investment is cultivated for maximum return. If the process undertaken by the church proves to be the problem, that process is refined out of respect for the student. Excellence in process as well as performance is the norm to which these churches aspire.

Third, students are respected through the goals established to drive the process. These goals are established on two levels. On the one hand the church, having the "big picture" of what Christian maturity entails, creates a systematic process designed to promote such maturity among students. This process identifies the desired outcomes and then prepares an educational and relational plan for achieving those outcomes. On the other hand, the church also works with each believer to develop an individualized plan that will enable the believer to approach complete spiritual maturity as quickly, comprehensively and reasonably as is feasible for the individual. The key to the success of this step is for the student to "own" both the necessity of personal spiritual development and the plan created toward fulfilling that end.

If this sounds as if it is a labor-intensive, time-consuming, interactive process, that's because it is! Highly effective churches are our most outstanding agencies of life transformation because they are so serious about facilitating spiritual maturity. They recognize that our culture resists such development through a myriad of obstacles that seek to redirect people's attention and resources. However, because they are so firm in their belief about the importance of spiritual formation, these churches do not hesitate to commit the human and tangible resources required to enable students to continue their march toward maturity.

THE ROLE OF THE TEACHER

The centrality of the student in this process in no way undermines the significance of the teacher. Godly, skilled teachers are indispensable in the spiritual development of Christians. These churches highly esteem their teachers, largely because they expect so much of them. And, of course, that means that highly effective churches are very selective about whom they endorse as teachers.

Based on my experience at these churches, I'd describe the role of the teacher as that of a tour guide rather than scholar. This is an important distinction. The teacher is expected to be more than just a conduit for the transfer of religious information; the teacher is a facilitator of learning not a lecturer dispensing facts to be memorized. Effective teachers are individuals who, themselves, possess a suitable degree of spiritual maturity, but whose major function is to guide a student along a path of discovery that is driven primarily by the student. This removes the burden of having and delivering complete spiritual knowledge from the shoulders of the teacher. Instead, the teacher must be sensitive to the overarching goals of the developmental process.

Such teachers are not an overabundant commodity. Highly effective churches recruit individuals to teach based upon spiritual gifts and spiritual maturity. Even then, teachers are intentionally prepared for success through significant investments in training. Highly effective churches have extensive mentoring and educational efforts designed to refine the teaching skills of their teachers. The average tenure of lay teachers at these churches far exceeds the norm, largely because the process ensures that the teachers themselves are always growing. The church's continual investment in its teachers bears significant dividends.

But the defined role of the teacher is also different at these churches. They are deemed to be part of the ministry team within the church. Teachers are not, as is the case in most Protestant churches, lone rangers who teach what they want, in whatever forum is available to them (Sunday School, small groups, elective classes), having unlimited permission to continue as long as they provide students with information that is biblically defensible. At the highly effective churches, the content taught is carefully determined in conjunction with the church leaders. The objective of this process is neither control nor perfection, but consistency with the larger ministry strategy that is being implemented by the church. The educational choices reflect the goals of the church, its developmental philosophy and its macrolevel understanding of the congregation and of what is and is not working within the developmental process.

You may recall previous studies that have noted that the fastest-growing churches are often the ones that demand the most of people. Even in a low-commitment culture such as ours, people struggle to understand parameters and possibilities. Churches—or any institutions, for that matter—that provide people with a clear sense of boundaries and provide opportunities for personal growth, achievement and success within those boundaries have a certain appeal. Granted, not all people are at a stage of their personal development where they are willing to embrace limits and specific goals. Millions and millions of Americans, however, are searching for meaning and purpose. An organization, such as a church, that can articulate an appropriate reason for such parameters and procedures becomes an attractive alternative in a culture rife with ill-developed, half-baked options. Highly effective churches attract and keep great lay teachers because they know what they stand for as a ministry, what a mature Christian looks like and the route that must be traveled to develop committed students.

THE PROCESS

Let me take the argument a step further by noting that these churches expect their people to commit to a long and intense spiritual development process. For instance, one of these churches does not allow people to apply for membership until they have completed a nine-month class regarding spiritual foundations. Another church requires that all new members enroll in a yearlong class on basic Christian theology, perspectives and life applications. This depth of commitment is quite typical among highly effective churches. It becomes clear pretty quickly that involvement in a highly effective church is not for the fainthearted or the weekend observer. These churches are serious about helping people to maximize their Christian faith.

The process itself is systematic. The church is intent upon bringing its people somewhere definable and significant. To get there the church demands a heavy commitment from participants, but it justifies such a commitment by delivering lifelong benefits that otherwise are not likely to be attained. Evaluative comments made by the people involved in these procedures invariably reflected gratitude, enthusiasm and a sense of significance about the process itself. Of course, I was speaking with the people who have persevered; undoubtedly many people fell by the wayside once the weight of the required commitment became real. But my sense is that a large proportion of the people who sign on for such involvement find it to be addictive—and life changing.

Let me add a final word about the philosophy behind the spiritual development process of these churches. To some extent, their approach is a response to what they see happening in congregations across the nation. Here are some of the perspectives embraced by many of the highly effective churches:

- Memorizing Bible passages is a necessary but insufficient process to produce mature believers;
- Reading the Bible and books about the Bible and Christian faith is a useful but inadequate approach to

spiritual development. Such reading must be joined
with directed interaction to achieve maximum results;
• The accumulation of Bible knowledge is of limited
value unless a person understands how to apply that
knowledge. Information without application equals
knowledge without impact;
• Religious information that is conveyed without the
benefit of an organizing framework and spiritual
worldview results in intellectual confusion and behav-
ioral paralysis. A beneficial spiritual development
process provides its participants with a biblical worldview that can consistently serve as a perceptual filter
on reality and a means of responding to circumstances, challenges and opportunities in a biblically
sound, consistent and strategic manner.

In short, the systematic theological development process
implemented by highly effective churches does not create clones;
it creates thinking Christians who are given the tools to respond
to reality in a way that is consistent with their faith. The process
becomes self-sustaining because it works.

Methods for Effective Spiritual Growth

To get a deeper understanding of the systematic theological
growth facilitated by highly effective churches, let's consider the
methods they use.

The approach to education and development revolves
around four core principles: specified goals, personalization,
variety and creativity. As noted earlier, this process is based on
detailed goals that the church has established as a means to
"perfecting" the student and growing a mature collection of

saints and upon goals that each student articulates and owns as the objective of involvement in the process. As is always the case, those goals must be measurable for them to be valid. For instance, you could identify "greater Bible knowledge" as a goal. But how do you know if a student has actually achieved that goal? It is a desirable but meaningless goal unless you have determined what the student knows initially and then have a means of measuring new knowledge attained that therefore represents growth.

Highly effective churches seek a balance of universal knowledge (insights that every Christian should possess) and personalized wisdom (insights that reflect the unique qualities of the student's life and goals). This requires a developmental plan that incorporates mass education (classroom lessons), experiences and one-on-one attention (mentoring, cell groups). The profit from such a strategy is demonstrated in the degree of transformation that characterizes so many of the people involved in the process. Since this approach speaks directly to the unique needs, character and opportunities of the individual, it produces greater results, thereby justifying the greater investment in the student.

The systematic theological development process is facilitated by reliance upon multifaceted tracks of activity. For instance, there are multiple goals, such as the transfer of accurate biblical information, the ability to accurately interpret such information, the ability to discern the underlying principles and the consistent application of such principles. There are multiple communication methodologies relied upon—lecture, discussion, visual media, literature, etc. This multitrack approach is necessary because people have different learning styles and because using a variety of methods reinforces both the process and the message.

Don't overlook the significance of the creativity integrated into these processes. This is not all heavy-handed note taking and studying. Highly effective churches emphasize "active learning." This means that they go beyond just using sermons, lectures and reading assignments. They value tactics such as role playing, simulation, service projects, strategic games, field trips and ministry adventures and group discussions as means to growth. One of the pastors described his church's strategy as "whatever method it takes, in whatever place we must implement it, to get our people to grow in spiritual stature."

A final comment on methods: Highly effective congregations rely on repetition as a means to maturity. Every believer is periodically reexposed to the foundational, basic truths and principles on which individual development relies. The purpose of such review is to enhance recall of the fundamental building blocks of the faith as well as to reinforce the significance of those elements. While some might perceive review to offer the student a period of respite from the pressure of constant growth, my experience was that these times of returning to the basics enabled students to see old truths through new eyes. Having learned new information and principles, undergone new experiences and discovered new procedures for interpreting reality, occasional reviews enabled the student to understand that information in a new light—resulting in further growth.

THE RESOURCES TO GET THE JOB DONE

Surprisingly, most of the highly effective churches use a patchwork of pedagogical resources in their developmental efforts. These churches are well aware of the published resources available for Christian education and often purchase curriculum, books, CD-ROM products, videos and other items. I was surprised to find, however, that those products are often used as models, supplements or background information for resources that the church develops to reflect its unique needs and program. Because they have a well-defined perspective of where they are going and what they want to achieve, these churches are not shy about breaking the mold to pioneer new ways of doing things.

This independent nature means that the church, as an organization, is perceived by teachers and students alike to be both the champion of the underlying philosophy of spiritual development as well as a supplier of growth resources. Whether it is the pastor, a Christian education specialist or a lay person who is smitten by the Christian formation process, these churches always have one or more people who are their "resource persons"—the equivalent of an information warehouse from which materials, information, ideas or contacts can be obtained. These invaluable individuals do more than simply dispense materials; they also serve as knowledgeable experts who help to shape the evolving growth process espoused by the church.

Consistent with their developmental philosophy, these churches also invest relatively heavily in their teachers. The types of resources and projects they invest in include the following:

- training to refine teaching skills and abilities;
- emphasizing the primacy of learning rather than teaching;
- enhancing the instructor's understanding of and commitment to people;
- strengthening the teacher's commitment to and articulation of truth;
- ensuring that teachers are well informed about Scripture and how to make it come alive, without compromise, in their cultural context;

- upgrading ability to teach the Bible, specifically;
- assisting teachers in living the principles they teach.

As you can see, this is miles beyond the "warm body plugging a hole in the program" approach to recruiting and maintaining teachers. The Christians in highly effective churches experience personal transformation because their church is committed to giving them systematic development experiences that have been carefully conceived, strategically implemented and studiously evaluated. The personal spiritual depth that characterizes people who attend these churches is no accident; it is an outcome that is planned for, invested in and accounted for.

NOTES
1. George Barna, *The Second Coming of the Church* (Nashville, TN: Word Books, 1998). For a discussion with statistical evidence of this contention see chapters 1, 2 and 9.
2. This insightful study can be examined in a series of reports entitled "Effective Christian Education: A National Study of Protestant Congregations" written by Peter Benson and Carolyn Eklin and produced by the Lilly Endowment (Indianapolis, IN) in 1990.

HOLISTIC
STEWARDSHIP

Mention the word "stewardship" to most Americans and what comes to their minds? Frankly, nothing. Stewardship is not a word most people know or use. However, it has become a religious term used frequently by churches in relation to financial management.

Highly effective churches use the term, too, but they apply it in a more global manner. Stewardship is a big issue in these ministries, but the term is used to address more than the wise allocation of money. They define stewardship in terms of managing all of the resources that have been entrusted to us by God. All things are His, but He has appointed us to be the guardians of His estate. We have free reign with those resources, but will ulti-

7

mately be held accountable to Him, by Him, according to the guidelines provided in the Bible.

Most of the highly effective churches I studied border on the fanatical in their promotion of the notion that there are no victims in life—we reap what we sow. That concept is especially valid when it comes to how we handle God's resources. These resources include our time, money, relationships, opportunities, material possessions and abilities.

Stewardship Integrated into Teaching

As you might expect, effective churches go to great lengths to integrate biblical perspectives and principles on stewardship into all teaching. The underlying motivation is that stewardship is a behavior, but like any behavior, it is driven by values and assumptions. Consequently, these churches work hard to include a stewardship mind-set into the various lessons taught within the church.

The pastors of these churches typically deliver one or more sermons every year that are specifically about tithing, giving, or financial stewardship. However, they do not abandon the concept of stewardship at that point. Many other sermons and messages include allusions to stewardship principles (both financial and nonmonetary stewardship). By incorporating stewardship concepts into lessons on other topics, the congregation is not only reminded about the breadth and importance of stewardship but is also exposed to ways of interrelating key faith perspectives of thinking and living in a comprehensively Christian manner.

I witnessed many creative ways of tying stewardship thinking into sermons and other teachings that had no overt connection to stewardship. Among those connections to which I have been exposed, either during visits or by listening to tapes of presentations at the highly effective churches, include the following:[1]

Stewardship of:	Scripture passages or incidents	References
Time	Paul writes canonical letters while in prison; Jesus' entire ministry takes less than 3 years; Paul uses his freedom to preach in Rome.	Eph., Phil., Col. Gospels Acts 28
Opportunities	Jesus preached in all the towns, healed diseases; Paul and Silas evangelize the jailer.	Matt. 9 Acts 16
Relationships	Jesus' three-year commitment to the disciples; Jesus' first encounter outside the tomb was with two women–Mary and Mary Magdalene; Jesus defends the woman who anointed Him; Jesus' friendship and mentoring of Nicodemus; Jesus instructs John to protect His mother.	Gospels Matt. 28 Mark 13 John 3 John 19
Material Possessions	Early Church shares its possessions; Ananias and Sapphira cheat the Church.	Acts 4 Acts 5
Health	Jesus heals the sick and diseased people.	various
Gifts and Abilities	Apostles organize themselves to meet needs; Paul exhorts Timothy to stand firm; Luke records Christian history with detail.	Acts 6 1 Tim. Luke, Acts
Knowledge	Stephen's speech outlining Jewish history; Jesus prepares the apostles for persecution.	Acts 7 Matt. 10
Money	Jesus pays the Roman tax.	Matt.17
Truth	Satan's temptations of Christ; confrontation over circumcision.	Matt. 4 Acts 15

Figure 7.1

One of the outgrowths of this approach is that highly effective churches raise more money on a per capita basis and have a higher rate of ministry participation than do most churches. These outcomes cannot be solely attributed to the stewardship emphasis; leadership, structure, theological development and establishment of a sense of belonging and community certainly affect such behaviors. However, the emphasis on holistic stewardship undoubtedly makes a significant contribution to this condition.

FUND-RAISING IS DONE DIFFERENTLY

Our research among people who donate money to churches and other non-profit organizations has shown that there are six primary motivations that lead people to contribute to churches and charities. Fund-raising has become so competitive, though, that it is not good enough to satisfy just one of those motivations. Before a donor is likely to contribute funds to a church or charity at least three of those six motivations must be satisfied.[2]

Highly effective churches do a good job of raising the money they need to implement their ministry plans, but they do not devote an unusual amount of energy or attention to fund-raising. They are effective in raising funds partly because they are aware of what motivates people to financially support a ministry and can effectively communicate how their church fulfills those donor expectations. In fact, we learned that effective churches typically provide their congregations with ample evidence of the compelling cause that the church represents and the impact that the church is having upon people's lives. The third (and subsequent) motivations that are specifically addressed by these churches vary considerably.

It is completely within character for all of these churches to emphasize their cause and impact in relation to financial stewardship. After all, these are ministries that have strong, visionary leaders motivating the body of believers to break out of the box and experiment with innovative ways of being significant agents of transformation. Having a solid grasp of their cause, as reflected in their commitment to a unique and attractive vision for ministry, is what has drawn people to these churches and cemented their commitment to it. And the very notion of transformation is indistinguishable from the concept of impact.

To their credit, highly effective churches never assume that they can simply expect people to give to the church. Gone are the days when church-going people understand, much less produce tithing. Less than 5 percent of the church-going population tithes these days. Most people who attend a church provide financial assistance, but it is often quite limited—donations that amount to less than $10 per week among regular attenders and substantially less among sporadic attenders.

To combat the possibility that people might regard donating to the ministry as an optional behavior, even after sermons that address the financial obligations and opportunities of a Christian, the leaders of these churches intentionally address the ministry endeavors that speak to the issues that motivate people to donate.

In these churches the senior pastor is not the primary fundraiser. This is a strategic choice these churches have made. The underlying reason is their experience—and our research that confirms that experience—suggesting that productive fundraising and effective pastoring are like mixing oil and water. Fundraising in many instances cripples a minister's ability to pastor because the people are never quite sure of the motivation of the pastor's words or actions. "Did the pastor preach that message because it's the right thing to teach and it contains important principles for us to embrace or because it will raise more money which is needed to pay his/her salary?" "Is the pastor spending time with me because he/she really cares for me or because it will make it harder for me not to donate generously when the stewardship campaign arrives?"

The leader/pastors of highly effective churches serve as key, strategic decision-makers in the overall stewardship activities of the church without taking on the role of asking the congregation to give. As an integral member of a stewardship team the leader can interject important biblical and practical suggestions for the team to consider. The leader/pastor can also serve as a

A hallmark

of highly

effective

churches is

accountability.

cheerleader to the congregation, thanking them for their generosity when such encouragement is warranted, or moving the congregation to prayerfully consider the financial condition of the church and their personal role in facilitating the ministry and its vision.

Another dynamic role the pastor can play is that of model steward. Because such a large portion of what people learn is absorbed through observation, the way in which the senior leader of the church comports himself/herself in the stewardship realm will speak more loudly than a half dozen well-preached sermons on generous giving practices.

ALWAYS ACCOUNTABLE

As mentioned previously, a hallmark of highly effective churches is *accountability.* Naturally, these churches have discovered ways to hold their people accountable to maintain generous giving, but without being overbearing or intrusive. Some of the ways in which they accomplish this include:

- having the stewardship team held accountable for meeting its deadlines and reaching its goals;
- holding each ministry, department and program within the church to its budget;
- keeping the congregation informed about the financial condition of the church through correspondence, handouts at church and public announcements, so that people have an accurate sense of the church's financial condition;
- having the stewardship representatives in the church, each of whom is a lay person typically responsible for interacting with a limited number of congregants regarding the finances of the church, stay in close contact with every person to whom they are assigned to answer special questions and to provide "soft" accountability for each person's giving;
- providing periodic pledge updates/reminders to those individuals who had pledged to give a specified amount during the year;
- having meetings between attenders and a responsible leader who has access to the giving records of the church body and can skillfully and sensitively address the lack of financial support shown by those attenders.

I did find that although talking to congregants about donations is a matter that raises great trepidation among most pastors, it is a nonissue to the leader/pastors of highly effective churches. One pastor remarked:

Do I relish conversations with members about the fact that they don't give? Actually, I do, because their *failure to support us financially is simply indicative of deeper spiritual problems* they have. Sometimes it's a lack of understanding about biblical stewardship but sometimes I learn that they have personal financial needs that we can help them with through a gift, a loan or budgeting assistance. Sometimes they're battling a spirit of selfishness. Often it's simply their unwillingness to trust God or take Him at His word.

This pastor intrigued me because, like so many of his peers in the highly effective churches, he seemed to treat fund-raising as if it were no more intimidating than helping the choir decide what hymns to sing next Sunday or what color to have the fellowship hall repainted. His people give at nearly twice the per capita average.

A lot of that church's financial security has to do with this pastor's approach to people and their giving and to the quality of the laity he has serving as the stewardship facilitators of the church. He went on to say:

I don't look at my conversations with people who are not giving to the church as if I'm the bill collector coming to repossess the family's house. I think of myself as a scout who has been sent out in advance of an approaching dignitary, like a king or general, to tell people they'd better get ready, the Man is coming. I don't enter those conversations with the intent of forcing anyone to give to the church. How could I possibly do that? But I do intend to carry out my personal responsibility as the spiritual leader of this Body to challenge the beliefs and behavior of my people with all the courage, sensitivity and wisdom I can muster.

Once again, even as we discuss a substantive issue such as stewardship, the answer comes back to leadership. Casting an appropriate vision to motivate people to give and to live as effective stewards makes a huge difference. Incorporating stewardship into public messages conveyed to the congregation is a strategic act—a leadership act. Focusing people on the big picture of Christian practice—accomplished in this case by expanding people's view of stewardship beyond money management to embrace total life and resource management—is characteristic of leaders. The ultimate result of this strategic leadership emphasis is that churchgoers are more knowledgeable about their faith, more obedient to God through the practice of holistic stewardship and the church is a more effective agent of transformation.

NOTES

1. These relate to the New Testament examples I can recall. There were a number of Old Testament examples as well. My purpose here is not to give an exhaustive listing of possibilities, but simply an idea of how some teachers have correlated well-known Bible stories with the concept of holistic stewardship.

2. The six motivations are the desire to be part of a compelling cause; the desire to make a lasting difference in the world; the expectation of receiving a personal benefit from the work done by the organization; the existence of a significant relationship with people of influence within the organization or with a group of donors who support the organization; the desire to help meet an urgent need being addressed by the organization; and the appeal of the organization's efficiency in its operations. For a more detailed discussion of these matters see *How To Increase Giving in Your Church* by George Barna, (Ventura, CA: Regal Books, 1997).

SERVING THE COMMUNITY

Several years ago we conducted a nationwide survey among people who never attend church. We asked many questions including what types of churches would be most appealing to them if that they decided to visit a church. One of the most common responses was they would seek a church that was committed to helping people outside the church who needed care and consideration.

In recent years, with government cutbacks in services and pressure to balance government budgets, much debate has ensued around the importance of churches picking up the slack in addressing the needs of people who will no longer be assisted by the government. The government increasingly relies upon churches to support those who fall through the cracks of our society. Even though many legislators and government officials do not wish to grant churches government recognition or favor, they believe that churches are an indispensable part of the social support system in America.

In another national survey we conducted among a random sampling of adults, we asked what they felt were the most important reasons for churches to exist. Among the most frequent answers provided was to demonstrate the love of God by helping the needy. Even adults at large deem social service ministry to be one of the most significant contributions of the church. In short, most adults expect churches to serve the needy.

Unfortunately, we have also discovered that churches talk a better game than they live when it comes to social service ministry. A pair of surveys we conducted late in 1998 showed that more than four out of five senior pastors claim their churches are "consistently engaged in serving the poor and needy in the community." These signs of encouragement do not tell an accurate story of the compassion of our churches, though. For instance, we also found budgets for community ministry are slim to invisible in all but the most unusual of churches. Further, realize that a minority of churchgoers volunteer their services to their church—and very few of those people invest themselves in ministry geared to people outside of the congregation. We also found that fewer than 1 out of every 10 Protestant churches had worked in cooperation with another church in their area to accomplish parallel ministry goals.

Put this all together and we have a nation with tens of thousands of churches that give little more than lip service to community service. Perhaps that is what makes the commitment of highly effective churches to the needy among us so discernible. And perhaps this same commitment also helps to explain why many people are attracted to these churches.

Striking a Balance

As much as highly effective churches are dedicated to meeting the needs of people outside their community of faith, even those churches struggle to maintain a reasonable balance between focusing on the needs of congregants and addressing the needs of outsiders. "In our fellowship we see-saw back and forth," was the way the pastor of a rapidly growing church in the Southwest described his situation. He continued:

> Our people have big hearts, but they also have a desire to have their own needs met. So we're always going back and forth, shifting our resources to accommodate the needs of the moment. It's a bit taxing on our leaders because it's not as stable and predictable as you'd like, but then again, good ministry is always pretty unpredictable. We just try to be sensitive to where things are at any given moment and remain flexible enough to do the best we can for the greatest number of people.

That philosophy is indicative of the dynamic tension that most of the effective churches face: meeting congregational needs versus meeting community needs. One leader explained:

> We try to comfort our people by reminding them that both groups of people—those in the church and those on the outside—are of equal importance, but that the needs we address will not necessarily receive equal emphasis. We'll probably always put more of our time and energy into helping the people in the church. The hurdle is how much is appropriate to devote to those you want to love into the kingdom.

So like most of the effective churches, this pastor's congregation has an unequal balance of resources allocated to each group, with the majority of ministry resources committed to ministry received by the congregation. However, that resource allocation equation is in a permanent state of flux, reflecting the ever-present frustration of never having enough resources to meet all of the identifiable needs in the their midst.

I was most impressed, though, by the fundamental perspective that drives the social concern of the effective churches: "You cannot become completely healthy until you get your eyes off of yourself and onto others." In their eyes, a church that allows itself to become too self-absorbed is simply unhealthy.

In fact, several of the effective congregations studied were classic "turnaround churches"—bodies that went from great strength to a period of collapse and then arose from the scrap pile to become vibrant ministries once again. The experience of each of the resurrected churches was that an exaggerated emphasis upon outreach rather than inreach is what restored vitality.

EXPANDING THE COMFORT ZONE

Everyone develops personal comfort zones within which they operate. Those comfort zones are not harmful—unless they become so solidified that they preclude personal growth. The highly effective churches, in the desire to strike an ever-changing but viable balance between inreach and outreach, seek to have their people continually expanding or at least reshaping their ministry comfort zones.

Highly effective or not, these churches are hard-pressed to get their people to accept the constant expansion concept. It's not because these people are not committed to Christianity or to ministry or that they have no ownership of ministries of compassion. The issue is one of pain. Personal growth requires change; change creates discomfort; being human, people naturally attempt to avoid hardship, suffering, pain or discomfort of any type. And the truth is, community service ministries are often among the most difficult from which to achieve positive results. Ministries among the poor, the abused, the divorced, the disabled, the terminally ill and so forth are ministries requiring patience and perseverance—qualities that wear thin pretty quickly for many people.

Highly effective churches combat people's tendency to avoid the discomfort of personal growth by creating an environment that makes such growth virtually inescapable. It seems that these bodies usually follow a four-step process to facilitate influential community service ministry:

1. they give permission and encouragement to engage in social service ministry;
2. they allow their people to grow through experience, including the option of "failing with dignity";
3. they position people's shortcomings in service ministry as a process of discovery;
4. they motivate their people to continue to engage in service ministry, even if their prior experience was unsuccessful.

They then repeat steps two through four until their people become expert in their ministry, and provide those successful service ministers opportunities to encourage and train others to embrace service ministry.

At every step along this path—even in the wake of misspent money, unproductive time, or disappointing results—the lay ministers were applauded for their efforts and encouraged to hang tough. Rather than focus on inadequate results, these churches find ways to build up their lay ministers, including acknowledgment of the fact that some of Jesus' own ministry efforts did not appear to bear positive, tangible results.

Sometimes the pastors of these churches resort to inspirational conversations with these lay workers.

"Remember, Jesus calls us to be obedient, not perfect," explained one pastor of a small church that is heavily involved in community service projects. "The apostles weren't too competent while under Jesus' wing, yet He never removed them from active ministry because of their failure to achieve absolute excellence. If God looks at the heart, then I think we have some room to make mistakes as we reach out to serve the community. But it's important to remind our members that the goal here is to do what's right, regardless of the outcomes."

The pastor of a midsized church in Texas was even more direct about his support for the sometimes-unproductive service attempts of his congregation.

We try to help the homeless, the abused, single moms and also immigrants who don't speak English. This isn't easy. Sometimes my people get discouraged because they don't see overnight success or because the people we try to help don't want to be helped. What's most discouraging is when they hear other believers criticizing them for doing a less-than-perfect job. I even had another pastor in town call me up and ask me to get our people to stop ministering to homeless people because he thought we were doing it all wrong. So I asked the brother, "We'd love to learn how to be more effective. How do you help the homeless?"

"Well, we don't," was his answer.

So I told him, "Then I'd rather help them my way than not help them your way." Honestly, I'm proud that this little group of people hasn't given up on helping hurting folks. That's what the church is supposed to be.

I might add that the failures experienced in community ministry by highly effective churches tend to fall into five categories: lack of training for the lay ministers, absence of adequate leadership, absence of a viable plan, insufficient funding and unrealistic expectations. While these are churches that believe a mistake is just another step along the road to success, they do insist on not repeating past mistakes. They always rectify these faults and rarely commit the same foible twice. One reason for their remarkable impact in community service ministries is that they are so diligent about learning from their past errors.

The reason for

the remarkable impact

highly effective

churches have

in community service

ministries is that

they are so diligent

about learning

from their

past errors.

MODELING BY LEADERS

Naturally, the best way of exhibiting the importance of serving the community and the acceptability of temporary failure as a means to improvement in the quality of performance and long-term impact, is for the leaders of the church to accompany the laity in service ministry. Pastors can preach all year about the importance of taking risks and how the church will support those who try and fall short—and perhaps never strike a resonant chord within congregants. But when they see a pastor, elder or ordained staff person taking a bold risk, falling flat, getting up, growing and eventually succeeding—with the encouragement and uninterrupted support of the church—verbal exhortations to take risks become more than just the expected words. When leaders what it means to push the limits of their gifts, abilities and resources because of a need to be obedient to God's commands, then the people feel more comfortable about joining the fray.

In fact, one of the most significant lessons to emerge in relation to this habit was the importance of the church's leaders modeling firsthand involvement with the poor, the suffering, the lonely and other social outcasts to whom the love of Christ could be made real.

> For probably six or seven years I preached sermons regularly about getting outside of our cozy religious cocoon to help our neighbors in need. Nobody budged. In one of our monthly elders meetings I raised the challenge again, to deadly silence, and just reached my breaking point. I began asking them about their commitment to being all that God has called them to be, especially as leaders within the church. One of the men, bless his heart, had the courage to say what was on everybody's mind but nobody's lips. "Pastor, we're just wonderin', maybe you could tell us about how you help the poor folk in town and then we'll have a better idea of what you have in mind."

Bull's-eye! They caught me doing the holyman's lecture. I was stunned. At first I couldn't figure out if I was angry or embarrassed or just plain unfit to be a pastor. It was quiet for a while, before I realized that I had no right to bully them about something I hadn't lived in twenty years. Plain truth is, he was right. So we talked about starting down that road together. As a group, we committed to working in the community together. We did, and then the congregation caught wind of it and followed suit. I don't think I've preached a sermon since then—at least I hope I haven't—when I didn't check to make sure I wasn't asking them to do anything I hadn't already done. If I'm the leader, they have to see me doing the things I ask of them. If I haven't or cannot or won't do it, I shouldn't expect it of them.

Among the more intriguing approaches to Christian service adopted by some of the highly effective churches was the requirement that leaders must be actively involved in a service ministry. While this approach has produced some mixed results it has also sent a very clear message to the congregations: Leadership means serving others.

CREATING SYNERGY

To make the most of the unlimited opportunities to serve the world around them, highly effective churches often work in cooperation with other nearby churches to facilitate community service. Given their emphasis upon leadership and goals, this attitude is not surprising; they know they can accomplish more with capable partners than they can accomplish in isolation.

My exploration of the partnership aspect of highly effective churches found that there seems to be a commitment, sometimes articulated and sometimes not, to four dimensions of cooperative ministry.

- *Willingness to Teach*

  Highly effective churches are happy to act as a teaching body, in which they mentor people from other churches in aspects of service ministry that the successful church has mastered.

- *Willingness to Learn*

  When highly effective churches want to get involved in an area of community service they have never championed before, first they strive to learn from the churches who are more experienced in such a ministry. This reflects the willingness of effective churches to submit to others. While serving as an apprentice under the tutelage of smaller or different churches might put off some, servants from highly effective churches always seemed happy to learn from other Christians who were more experienced or more skilled.

- *Willingness to Serve*

  Highly effective congregations will work alongside churches or parachurch ministries which are neither as experienced nor professional in the ministry being undertaken. Again, this willingness to be an unheralded team member when they perhaps qualify as the "superstar" speaks to their controlled ego and their commitment to being part of the Body of Christ.

- *Willingness to Accept Differences*

  A focus on getting the job done properly supersedes

an effective church's need to work with partners who see everything the same way they do. I found effective congregations serving homeless people in partnership with parachurch ministries; helping single mothers in conjunction with secular, for-profit corporations; partnering with nonreligious, nonprofit organizations to assist abused children; and accepting government grants or working with government agencies to address the problems of handicapped people and poor people. They will work with virtually any partners who possess the same goals, even if their motivations are different.

The pastor of a midsized Baptist congregation in the Midwest addressed this commitment to serving the needy through unusual alliances.

Some of the guys in my denomination question why our church is working hand in hand with state agencies or with some of the local service groups that don't profess Christ as Lord. It's because we have been called to bless people. If I can work in partnership with a government agency and see people's lives mended and emotional wounds healed, that's God at work, not a government agency. I want some of that action; God will use any instrument He desires to get His will accomplished. I'm not going to cheat my congregation out of great opportunities to serve the community because we don't see eye to eye on every issue with a potentially helpful partner. I'd rather see people helped and take part in that than to be self-righteous and isolated from reality.

EQUIPPING
THE FAMILY

L eo Tolstoy once wrote, "All happy families resemble one another; every unhappy family is unhappy in its own way." In some respects, the families in highly effective churches resemble each other. I believe the reason is that those churches have a completely different perspective on family ministry than do most churches.

Building up Christian families is one of the most desperately needed—and most daunting—challenges facing the Church today. Every day the mass media provide new and frightening evidence of the dissipation of emotionally healthy families as well as the demise of the values and lifestyles typically associated with such families. Behaviors such as divorce, homosexual relationships, cohabitation and giving birth without marriage have become commonplace in America. Meanwhile, there are signs that as our culture continues to reinvent itself, and the role of churches is further challenged and repositioned, the family unit will play a much more significant role—perhaps even the dominant role—in the spiritual growth of the family's members. We must therefore determine how well prepared families are to handle the increasing pressures, temptations and ministry opportunities that will be cascading upon them.

Sadly, it seems that families are already buckling under today's pressures and anxieties; relatively few families seem adequately equipped to take on more. Our data suggest that perhaps one out of every five families is emotionally healthy and functioning productively. Another segment, perhaps about one-third of all families, have their ups and downs but generally get by okay. The other half, however, are truly struggling with family life. Communication, sexuality, finances and a host of other challenges are overwhelming many families—most of which feel they have no support system or background that enables them to rise to meet each challenge.

Fortunately, there is ample evidence that if churches are willing to consider a new paradigm of family ministry, it is possible to appropriately equip them. The highly effective churches are blazing new paths in this wilderness.

What Do Families Need?

Our nationwide surveys with parents have identified seven primary needs of families. In brief form, here are those seven perceived needs.

1. Trustworthy Counselors

When pressed, most parents admit that they have not developed a comprehensive, practical philosophy of family and parenting that helps them handle the myriad of family-oriented choices and decisions they must make. There is a deep yearning across America for parenting or family mentors who will serve as a safe sounding board in relation to the uncertainties and difficulties facing parents. Ideally, such counselors would be experienced and nonjudgmental and would employ a Socratic-based style to nudge parents forward. The need for such mentors is underscored by the content of the prevailing philosophy of family success, which can best be described as "making it through another day." Regardless of good intentions, most parents have not thought through their views on their goals and strategies for having a viable family.

2. A True Partnership in Marriage
Divorce rates are still climbing, but that is, of course, a symptom of the real problem, which is the absence of a symbiotic love relationship between the husband and wife. A large proportion of married adults state that their spouse is their best friend and that they would marry the same person if they had a chance to start over. Yet there is a deep undercurrent of frustration among married adults based on the feeling that they and their spouse are not on the same page with regard to their relationship, the raising of their kids, and the post-children life the couple hopes to lead. Experiencing a relationship that is balanced and appropriately focused is a dream harbored by many married Americans.

3. Better Child Development Skills
Most parents want to inculcate positive, lasting foundations in the minds of their children, but have no idea

how to strategically accomplish the task. The three elements they most desire to introduce to their young people are appropriate moral values, self-esteem and methods of handling extreme emotions. The concern of millions of American parents is that they only address these issues when a crisis arises in their child's life—and that the recommended response is random or situational. Sadly, most parents don't know an alternative approach and are hoping someone can identify one for them.

4. Better Parenting Skills

Most parents believe that parenting is their greatest responsibility in life and that the way their kids turn out will represent their major legacy. The problem is that they have never received any training or preparation for the task. There are five particular areas of parenting for which they seek greater help. One is better communication between husband and wife as well as between parent and child. Another felt need is knowing how to convert the home into a positive learning environment. A third desire is to understand how to resolve conflicts. Fourth, establishing priorities and managing time effectively are significant needs. The final skill desired is financial planning and management. The positioning of the assistance provided is also crucial. Parents tend to resist desirable training if it is labeled "basic parenting skills."

5. Greater Courage to Change

Most parents know they are in a parenting rut—they do the same things over and over and feel powerless to change the behaviors that they know are inadequate responses to their children's or family's needs. Sadly, most of them conclude that they have neither a plausible strategy for change nor the courage to implement the necessary degree of change. Tired of repeating the same inadequate behaviors, they desire a mechanism that can provide direction and bolster their confidence in adopting that solution.

6. Greater Emotional Support

Families are in a seemingly constant state of stress and confusion. Decades ago the coping mechanism was the extended family; relatives were available to relieve some of the pressure from the parents. With the extended family living on its own these days, parents have to deal with family stress in isolation. Most parents therefore are looking for individuals, groups, organizations or techniques that will provide better emotional support to help them get through times of family stress, confusion or anxiety.

7. A Family-Crisis Safety Net

When stress or conflict gets out of control, crisis occurs. The notion of a safety net is one in which physical security, emotional support, spiritual clarity and relational empathy are provided for parents in the midst of the family implosion. For a large percentage of people, their church is the only source of such a safety net. Their tenuous ties with their church, however, make this source of security seem less secure than they would like.

We interviewed a large national sample of teenagers on the same issue. The results show that teens have some very strong feelings about family—specifically, they desperately want to have a happy, tightly knit, loving family, but feel many things must change for that to exist. Young people provided their own list of changes that they feel must occur in order to have a positive family lives. The most widely coveted changes included these:

- a deeper sense of belonging to and unconditional love from their family;
- better communication with their parents;
- more time spent with their parents in meaningful interaction (i.e., more than being in the same room watching television together—which is currently the dominant "shared experience");
- receiving genuine respect from their parents;
- their parents acceptance of the teen's peers;
- greater emotional closeness among family members;
- their parents showing deeper respect and tolerance for each other;
- less financial stress for the family;
- greater physical safety or protection against crime.

The stated needs of parents and of teenagers—and the gap between their respective needs—indicate that families seem mired in a perpetual state of flux and redefinition. While that is not necessarily bad, it does suggest that there is also an ongoing need for a variety of types of support to facilitate the proper development of the family.

The Role of the Church

Christian churches have long been friendly to families. A huge majority of churchgoers contend that their church cares deeply about the state of families and does whatever it can to support families. The issue confronting churches then is not whether they are perceived to be family-friendly but whether they are seen as providing practical and valuable help to families.

Survey data suggest that Americans are not convinced that churches are doing much to truly help families. Most people admit that Protestant churches are doing a good job of teaching biblical principles about family, offering Christian-based counseling services to families that are experiencing crisis, encouraging people to strive for a family that is consistent with biblical norms, and praying for the need of families and their children.

However, consider the areas that most church people say have eluded the church. Most adults say that churches fare poorly at facilitating meaningful relationships within families as well as among the family units in the church. Most claim that even though the church professes to care, theirs does not regularly check up on families to ensure that they are getting the attention and resources necessary to be effective and healthy. Even larger majorities claim that their church does not adequately provide family development resources or role models.

The track record of the church in supporting families does appear somewhat checkered. But further analysis also shows the tremendous potential that churches have for connecting with and empowering families. For instance, churches have the highest credibility among all of the institutions and organizations that focus on helping families. Further, churches enjoy the advantage of having the most frequent and regular contact with families. Few organizations have such access to families. Perhaps most valuable though is the church's image in regard to family assistance. Most Americans expect churches to help families. That is invaluable; it opens the door for churches to build trust-based, solution-driven relationships with families.

Key Family Ministry Principles

Highly effective churches have been among the most successful at exploiting the need for faith-based answers to the questions raised by families. Our research revealed that there are nine principles implemented by these churches that enable them to move beyond maintenance and into life-changing ministry. Each highly effective church applied these principles in a different way, producing a body of effective churches that generate similar results but through very divergent ministries. The beauty of their approach to families is that it is simple, biblical and transferable. Here are the cornerstones of their approach to building strong families.

EQUIPPING THE FAMILY FOR SELF-DEVELOPMENT

Make no mistake about it, this is the single most important principle of the entire family development approach embraced by highly effective churches. All of the other principles lose their power if they are not built upon this cornerstone.

Highly effective churches believe that for a family to be healthy and functional, it must possess the tools required to completely address the various challenges, opportunities or conditions that are likely to face the family. This means that the task for the church is to teach a family to identify its own needs and how to meet them, to provide families with the skills and knowledge required to meet those needs and to help families achieve the self-confidence required to implement solutions.

This represents a radical reconceptualization of ministry to families. The prevailing model in churches is to attract families by offering as many family-oriented programs and ministries as possible and to have specialists employed by the church who will solve family problems through those programs. Highly effective churches argue that such an approach actually cripples families because it creates a dependency upon the church to solve family problems. Instead of giving families responsibility for their own issues, it places the responsibility on the church which then prevents the family from being independent, self-sustaining and healthy.

I suspect that the prevailing family ministry model is an outgrowth of one of the major problems in churches: the determination to have control over people's lives. This is evident in churches where the pastor is not a leader, where there is defective theology or where staff members are evaluated on inappropriate performance criteria. The beauty of the highly effective church model is that it redefines the role of the church from that of the primary deliverer of services to that of a support system. In other words, the church enables families to minister to themselves instead of doing the required ministry to the family.

Highly effective churches have flourished under this philosophy. They are freed from the impossible

Highly effective churches

enable families

to minister to themselves

instead of doing

the required ministry

to the family.

burden of having to save families from themselves. Instead, they become a compassionate resource to families. Most of the highly effective churches do not have a staff person whose job is to focus on family needs; such positions often trap a church in the old style of ministry, motivating the staff person to justify his/her salary by proving that the church successfully solves family problems. Highly effective churches that do have a staff member dedicated to family development expect these specialists to serve as resource people rather than miracle workers.

CLEAR STANDARDS

Like most churches, the highly effective congregations provide people with clear and specific biblical standards regarding family. In today's culture there are many competing philosophies about family and it is easy, if not inevitable, for a family to become confused and enticed by those various views. Highly effective churches return to a traditional role of the church: provide people with information from the Bible as to what a family is, how it should function and the inescapable consequences of rejecting God's views on family.

These standards allow families to behave in ways that are based on truth rather than cultural norms, current fads or personal whims. They also facilitate the independence of the family, giving it the ability to make its own decisions and address its needs without having to rely upon pastors and other church officials for solutions. When the family sufficiently understands the Bible and its dictates for family life, it is better equipped to avoid crises and to handle those which arise.

GOALS AND PLANS

It has been said that an entity that fails to plan plans to fail. That axiom gains credibility in the realm of family life. Fewer than four percent of today's families have set specific goals and related plans for themselves. The result is quite obvious: Lacking concrete direction, the tacit goal becomes survival. According to national divorce statistics which show America to have the highest divorce rate in the developed world, we are not even accomplishing that minimal goal.

Highly effective churches never tell a family what its goals should be. They motivate families to develop goals and plans so that the family can succeed on its own. These churches give families information, models, encouragement, procedural assistance and assessment tools. They direct families to consider the kinds of goals that would strengthen and develop their family in the spiritual, emotional, intellectual, physical and relational dimensions of life. The ultimate test of those goals and the related plans is simple: Will the goal honor God and will it mature the family?

Accountability for reaching those goals is one of the necessary facets of this developmental strategy. After all, if you don't specify a goal, you won't pursue it; if you don't intentionally pursue it, you won't measure it; and if you don't measure it, you won't achieve it, except by accident. One of the family goals of highly effective churches is to eliminate reliance upon accidental success.

ADDRESSING NEEDS OF THE ENTIRE FAMILY

Many churches do their best to help families but their methods require the family to be split up: Adults are in one track, teens and adolescents in another, younger children in yet another track. (Some churches even divide mothers and fathers into different tracks because of doctrinal assumptions.) Our studies show that this slice-and-dice approach to developing family cohesion is counterproductive. Rather than building a unified family, it fosters the notion that the family is irreconcilably divided by age (and perhaps gender).

Highly effective churches work hard to give families opportunities to stay together for teaching, interaction and experiences. Given a root philosophy that maintains families should address their own needs rather than having a church solving their problems for them, such unity is integral to the desired end product. Frankly, this is one of the elements of family ministry that the highly effective churches struggle with the most. Creating ways of supporting all family members simultaneously is difficult. It appeared to me that the key is maintaining the perspective of enabling, not doing; in other words, the church's responsibility is to provide families with the tools, and let the families use the tools.

The family ministry of these churches therefore balances the provision of information and skills with opportunities for the family to experiment and grow. This is active education—experiences are an integral part of the process. Allowing families to fail as they test their abilities is one of the unique strategies of highly effective churches. If the church has done its job well then that failure maybe a helpful step toward the strengthening of the family. With the encouragement and mentoring of the church, that family will discern the failure, learn from it, make another attempt and grow from the entire episode.

DIVERSIFIED APPROACHES

Different people learn in different ways. Some grow best through lectures, some from hands-on experimentation, some from observation. Some people are visual learners, some are auditory learners, others are interactive in style. Group learning motivates some but turns off others; individualized study is where it's at for some, but not for others. To exploit the potential resident in every developmental tactic, highly effective churches do their best to tailor the growth experience to the needs of their people.

This makes the entire process much more diverse and difficult than would be the case if the underlying developmental philosophy necessitated providing only a series of sermons or classroom lectures. Naturally, the difficulty of the approach is irrelevant to highly effective churches; their primary consideration is not the ease of administration but the quality of the end result. They work hard to understand how people learn and then develop their tactics accordingly.

A critical element in the customization approach is to reinforce key lessons through repetition. But rather than expose people to the same information multiple times through the same presentation techniques or experiences, these churches seek to achieve recall, comprehension and application by presenting the information through different methods. As educational research has shown, communicating the same body of information in disparate ways often increases retention and comprehension. These are two vital steps that ultimately facilitate the goal of highly effective churches—i.e., application leading to transformation.

MENTORS AND COACHES

One aspect of the personalization of the family development process is to identify and deploy mentors for families. Naturally, there are some families that resist working with a coach. Most, however, appreciate the input received from an experienced advisor. These mentors are not live-in taskmasters; they are external but interested counselors who keep in touch and offer guidance without meddling. Their job is not to "fix" the family, but to help it when help is both merited and desired.

Great mentors do not try to shape the family to fit a certain mold, but seek to raise up the family to be all that it can be. They seize teachable moments to provide useful, practical insight to the family. They encourage when necessary, but they are honest about their observations; anything less stunts rather than fosters family growth. They ultimately allow the family to push the relationship; the mentor does not insinuate himself in the life of the family unless invited to do so.

Church leaders keep an eye open for individuals who have the ability to mentor families. A significant role of the church is to know who such mentors could be, to enlist them as mentors, team them with appropriate families and support these mentors for the duration of their service in this special role. It did not take long to discover that even the highly effective churches are suffering from a dearth of family mentors. That is indicative of the weakened condition of families across the nation.

PASTORS AS ADVOCATES

The senior pastors of the highly effective churches operate as champions of families. They serve families by setting the church's ministry agenda with the family clearly in mind. The pastor also sets the tone for the church in regard to family ministry; the signals sent by the pastor regarding the family will largely determine the way in which church resources are allocated to helping families grow.

I found that a pastor who is supportive of families but remains relatively silent on family development has essentially undermined the potential for families to get their fair share of help from that ministry. In a competitive environment such as the church, a person of influence must serve as an advocate for a ministry if it is to have standing. In the highly effective churches that advocate was the senior pastor—i.e., the church's high-profile leader—because of the importance of the family.

SEEKING GOD'S BLESSING

Families need prayer. Highly effective churches address this need by praying with families, praying for families and praying about families regarding their strength and development. This prayer focus is an ongoing priority within these churches. Such prayer occurs both in their public services and outside of church-wide events.

One of the keys in this strategy is to enable families to build a family prayer life. Perhaps the most crucial aspect of this endeavor is getting the mother, the father or both parents together to own the necessity of being a family that prays in a serious manner. In filling its support role, the church then continues to encourage its families (and especially the family's prayer champion) to continually deepen its prayer commitment.

INSTITUTING EVALUATION

It was interesting to find so many of the highly effective churches using evaluation of the spiritual and emotional health of their families as a barometer of the overall health of the church itself. This speaks volumes about the importance attached to families in these churches. The message this approach sends is very simple: As go our families, so goes our church.

Why evaluate the health of families? What the church does matters, but the church will have no idea how effective it is or how it can better accomplish its ends, unless it has a means of discovering the current state of affairs. Highly effective churches regularly take the pulse of the church—the solidarity of marriages, the communication levels within homes, the financial solvency of households, the spiritual activity among family members and so forth—to determine how to best support its families. Without such field intelligence all ministry efforts are a shot in the dark. Working in response to such knowledge, however, the church stands a far better chance of providing the kinds of assistance and support that will truly enhance family health and development.

Unspeakable Truths

Our research found that various realities impact the ability or approach to implementing this form of family ministry. Recognizing the limitations and opportunities created by those realities has enhanced the ministry activities of highly effective churches and facilitated a more appropriate interpretation of what families are experiencing in these churches. Here are a few of those realities.

PARENTS ARE VERY SENSITIVE ABOUT THEIR FAMILY'S IMAGE.

Consequences of this concern include the fact that parents will not attend a seminar offering "basic parenting skills" since attending a seminar with such a title would imply that they are incompetent parents. Positioning and image are critical aspects of developing an effective family ministry.

ACCOUNTABILITY MUST BE HANDLED CAREFULLY.

Parents completely endorse the notion of their children being accountable for their thoughts, words and deeds. However, when it comes to holding the family, through the parents, accountable for its development, many parents are terrified. Again, it is an image concern: What would happen if other people knew the truth about the family, and were exposed to all of the family's blemishes and faults? The prevalent response by highly effective churches has been to ensure that they introduce "soft accountability"—ways of assessing how the family is doing that are private, relational and in context. This is typically accomplished with one trusted confidant such as a mentor or through interaction with other families within the church. Accountability then becomes helpful rather than a threatening judgment.

WOMEN ARE THE KEY TO SUCCESS.

Despite all the recent efforts to heighten the responsibility men take for family leadership, the truth is that women remain the ones who will push for family development. That may not be what we want, but that's simply the way it is today so highly effective churches work with it. This impacts the way churches market their family ministry endeavors and how they provide needed services to families.

VALUED FAMILY MINISTRY CREATES OTHER MINISTRY OPPORTUNITIES.

If the church can prove its sincere concern and tangible value to the family, parents are more likely to invest themselves in the life of the church and in ministry efforts. This is reminiscent of the adage "hungry stomachs have no interest in the gospel," meaning that until a people's most pressing needs are addressed they will remain oblivious to other information and opportunities related to other needs, no matter how absolutely important they are. Family ministry is the same. Because of the pain or hardships that family life represents for so many Americans, unless the church can adequately address family issues, family members won't take the rest of the church's agenda seriously. However, once the church has brought about positive change for the family then the church's other concerns become of greater interest to family members. Earning their trust by delivering helpful ministry is instrumental in integrating them into extended ministry.

In the end, highly effective churches have learned that enhancing family life requires more than sermons and programs. The best approach is to provide families with the opportunities and skills they need to grow in their ability to implement God's principles by themselves. The church plays the role of equipping families to understand and implement those standards and to encourage and celebrate families in their journey. Breaking the cycle of codependence is not easy; transferring responsibility for family health from the church back to the family is a monumentally difficult but freeing and empowering endeavor.

——— # BECOMING HIGHLY EFFECTIVE

A fter presenting the nine habits of highly effective churches to an auditorium filled with pastors, one approached
me and exclaimed, "You've just described the perfect
church! My church could never be like that." I tried to correct two
of his misconceptions: that there is a "perfect" church and that
his church could never join the ranks of the highly effective congregations in America.

Perhaps you have read the preceding chapters and felt as that
pastor did—overwhelmed by the ability of highly effective churches to fight the good fight on all fronts. But do not misunderstand
my point. *These are not perfect, error free churches.* They are populated
by fallen human beings who have inappropriate emotions, develop
questionable relationships, waste money, use their time ineffi-
ciently, forget key biblical principles when making important decisions and do the right thing for the wrong reason—or sometimes
the wrong thing for the right reason. In other words, they are
churches just like yours and mine. What may distinguish them
from most churches is their ability to rise above setbacks, failings
and miscues to minister with competence and integrity, to finish

the ministry tasks they begin and to retain a laser-like focus on transformational ministry.

The highly effective churches we studied have numerous blemishes. But if we were to evaluate them on a scale of 1 to 10, with a rating of 10 representing excellence in the ministry dimension in question, the highly effective churches would be at the 9 or 10 mark in relation to most of the nine habits described in this book. For the few dimensions on which they were not at the positive end of the scale, they were in the process of diligently enhancing their performance in relation to those underdeveloped habits.

Not surprisingly, it became apparent that it is much easier to become highly effective if you are working with a new church (one that has not yet developed bad habits or become entrenched in routines) than if you are seeking to improve the habits of an older church. However, among the highly effective churches we discovered were some that had been through a prolonged period of ministry disaster but were able to turn around their ministry to achieve excellence and impact. Other churches showed that even without going through the throes of despair and dissipation, an older church may become renewed and transition from a survival-oriented church to a highly effective ministry. The key issue in both of these instances is leadership.

The Path to Becoming Highly Effective

No matter what the background of your church may be, however, becoming a highly effective ministry is never easy. Yes, you can visit some of these churches, observe what they do and how they do it and leave with confidence that you could easily do what they do—perhaps even better. But the great ones always make things look easy.

Some pastors make preaching seem effortless—until you try to develop a biblically sound, convincing and appealing message that speaks to people of all ages, backgrounds and needs. You don't see the years of theological training, the hours and hours of study, the sweat on Saturday night when a speaker can't find an illustration that fits, or the agonizing over how to communicate a deep theological issue in ways that first-time visitors can understand.

Some pastors make leadership of a dynamic ministry seem like a cakewalk—until you start to deal with multiple staff, hundreds of congregants with serious needs, divisive conflict among the elders, media pressures and the complacency that threatens to engulf any "successful" ministry. And you may never see the strain of making tough decisions, the anxiety brought about by conflict, the difficulty of juggling more tasks than can humanly be completed and the fear brought on by the debt incurred by a volunteer organization. Rest assured, having been behind the curtain, there is a lot more to making a church highly effective than meets the eye.

On the other hand, while becoming highly effective is not likely to be easy, it certainly is achievable. If God has called your church into existence then you may be assured His intention is for the church to flourish and not to flounder. In His Word He assures us that He will never abandon us and that He will always provide what we need, when we need it, as we seek to do His will for His purposes. Does that mean that victory will come easily? It rarely does. Does that mean that the path to victory will be clear? It rarely is. Does that mean that we can sit back and wait until He makes miraculous things happen so that our church becomes highly effective? Absolutely not; He endowed us with brains, language, energy and many other resources so that we can apply ourselves to the challenges of ministry and—with His guidance and blessing—see His will and His people prevail.

WHAT IS YOUR DREAM?

In the end you must ask yourself: What is your dream for your church? Is it to be a place where leaders can lead people to victory? A church where people share the gospel in strategic and life-changing ways? A congregation that is deeply supportive of each other and where people's relationships with God and family are intimate? A ministry in which the structure that is developed is secondary to the ministry that it facilitates? A sanctuary for the family where parents and kids receive the love, training and resources they need to cultivate Christian maturity? A place where God is worshiped with integrity and sincerity? A spiritual center where learning about the Christian faith is paramount and people are completely devoted to applying the spiritual insights they glean? A community whose heart goes out to the needy and whose time and resources are committed to serving the poor and disadvantaged?

If that is the church you desire, your dream is to be part of a highly effective church. Yours is a dream about spiritual significance and life transformation. You are dreaming of the church the way it is meant to be—and, with your dedication, the way it will become. Yours is a dream that pleases God—a dream that He is pleased to bring into reality. Commit yourself to that end and trust Him to bless your efforts.

RESOURCES

Bibliography

Bandy, Thomas. *Kicking Habits*. Nashville: Abingdon, 1998.

Barna, George. *The Second Coming of the Church*. Nashville: Word Publishing, 1998.

———. *How to Increase Giving in Your Church*. Ventura, CA: Regal Books, 1997.

———, ed. *Leaders on Leadership*. Ventura, CA: Regal Books, 1997.

———. *Turning Vision Into Action*. Ventura, CA: Regal Books, 1996.

———. *The Index of Leading Spiritual Indicators*. Dallas: Word Publishing, 1996.

———. *Evangelism That Works*. Ventura, CA: Regal Books, 1995.

———. *Generation Next*. Ventura, CA: Regal Books, 1995.

———. *The Power of Vision*. Ventura, CA: Regal Books, 1992.

Bennis, Warren. *On Becoming a Leader*. Reading, MA: Addison Wesley, 1989.

Bennis, Warren, and Goldsmith, Joan. *Learning to Lead*. Reading, MA: Addison Wesley, 1997.

Bennis, Warren, and Nanus, Burt. *Leaders*. San Francisco: HarperCollins, 1985.

Benson, Peter. *All Kids Are Our Kids*. San Francisco: Jossey-Bass Publishers, 1997.

Black, Thom. *Born to Fly*. Grand Rapids, MI: Zondervan, 1994.

Collins, James, and Porras, Jerry. *Built to Last*. New York: Harper Business, 1994.

Conger, Jay. *Learning to Lead*. San Francisco: Jossey-Bass, 1992.

Crabb, Larry. *Connecting*. Dallas: Word Publishing, 1997.

Dobson, James. *Solid Answers*. Wheaton, IL: Tyndale House, 1997.

Easum, William, and Bandy, Thomas. *Growing Spiritual Redwoods.* Nashville: Abingdon, 1998.

Ford, Leighton. *Transforming Leadership.* Downers Grove, IL: InterVarsity Press, 1991.

Galinsky, Ellen. *The Six Stages of Parenthood.* Reading, MA: Addison Wesley, 1987.

Garmo, John. *Lifestyle Worship.* Nashville: Thomas Nelson, 1993.

Greeley, Andrew. *Faithful Attraction.* New York: Tor Books, 1991.

Hammer, Michael, and Champy, James. *Re-engineering the Corporation.* San Francisco: Harper Collins, 1993.

Handy, Charles. *The Age of Unreason.* Boston: Harvard Business School Press, 1989.

Hendricks, Howard. *Teaching to Change Lives.* Portland, OR: Multnomah Press, 1987.

Hybels, Bill, and Mittelberg, Mark. *Becoming a Contagious Christian.* Grand Rapids, MI: Zondervan, 1995.

Kotter, John. *A Force for Change.* New York: Free Press, 1990.

———. *Leading Change.* Cambridge, MA: Harvard Business School Press, 1996.

Kouzes, James, and Posner, Barry. *The Leadership Challenge.* San Francisco: Jossey-Bass, 1995.

Lewis, Paul. *The 5 Key Habits of Smart Dads.* Grand Rapids, MI: Zondervan, 1994.

Lewis, Paul, and Black, Thom. *30 Days to a Smart Family.* Grand Rapids, MI: Zondervan, 1997.

Lewis, Robert. *Real Family Values.* Gresham, OR: Vision House, 1995.

Maxwell, John. *Developing the Leader Within You.* Nashville: Thomas Nelson, 1994.

Mead, Loren. *Transforming Congregations for the Future.* Washington, DC: Alban Institute, 1994.

Miller, Donald. *Reinventing American Protestantism.* Berkeley: University of California, 1997.

Morgenthaler, Sally. *Worship Evangelism*. Peabody, MA: Zondervan, 1995.

Mueller, Walter. *Understanding Today's Youth Culture*. Wheaton, IL: Tyndale House, 1995.

Roehlkepartain, Eugene. *The Teaching Church*. Nashville: Abingdon, 1993.

Sample, Tex. *Hard Living People and Mainstream Christians*. Nashville: Abingdon, 1993.

Sanders, J. Oswald. *Spiritual Leadership*. Chicago: Moody Press, 1967.

Sawchuck, Norman, and Rath, Gustav. *Benchmarks of Quality in the Church*. Nashville: Abingdon, 1994.

Schaller, Lyle. *Strategies for Change*. Nashville: Abingdon, 1993.

Senge, Peter. *The Fifth Discipline*. New York: Doubleday, 1990.

Sider, Ronald. *One-Sided Christianity*. Grand Rapids, MI: Zondervan, 1993.

———. *Genuine Christianity*. Grand Rapids, MI: Zondervan, 1996.

Sjogren, Steve. *Conspiracy of Kindness*. Ann Arbor, MI: Vine Books, 1993.

Steinbron, Mel. *The Lay-Driven Church*. Ventura, CA: Regal Books, 1997.

Towns, Elmer. *10 of Today's Most Innovative Churches*. Ventura, CA: Regal Books, 1990.

Wagner, C. Peter. *The New Apostolic Churches*. Ventura, CA: Regal Books, 1998.

Warren, Rick. *The Purpose-Driven Church*. Grand Rapids, MI: Zondervan, 1996.

Webber, Robert. *Worship Old and New*. Grand Rapids, MI: Zondervan, 1994.

———, ed. *The Renewal of Sunday Morning Worship* (vol 3). Grand Rapids, MI: Hendrickson, 1993.

Wiersbe, Warren. *Real Worship*. Nashville: Thomas Nelson, 1986.

Wills, Garry. *Certain Trumpets*. New York: Simon & Schuster, 1994.

About the Author

George Barna founded the Barna Research Group, Ltd. in 1984. The company's vision is to provide current, accurate and reliable information in bite-size pieces, at reasonable cost, to ministry leaders so they can make strategic decisions. Among the major thrusts of the company's research are to challenge prevailing assumptions and to identify new opportunities for the Church to be the agents of transformation that God intends.

Barna Research has served a variety of clients since its inception. Many major corporations have turned to BRG for help including Visa, Disney, Prudential, Columbia House, The Associates and Ford Motor Company. Barna Research has also served many nonministry, nonprofit organizations including CARE, Easter Seals, United Cerebral Palsy, Boys & Girls Clubs and others. The company's forte, though, is helping Christian ministries. To date BRG has served more than 100 parachurch ministries and numerous churches. The client base has included Billy Graham, Compassion International, American Bible Society, Prison Fellowship, CBN, Robert Schuller Ministries, World Vision, Thomas Nelson Publishing, Salvation Army, Trinity Broadcasting, International Union of Gospel Missions, Youth for Christ, Campus Crusade, The Navigators, InterVarsity and many others.

Barna was raised in a Catholic family in the Northeast and graduated summa cum laude from Boston College. After managing political campaigns and conducting polls for various candidates, he earned two graduate degrees from Rutgers University and was awarded the Eagleton Fellowship. During his graduate training he went on a "search for God" and accepted Christ in 1979. He later received a doctorate from Dallas Baptist University.

Barna has written extensively on issues related to church dynamics, popular culture and faith. To date, he has had more than two dozen books published, with several forthcoming volumes. Among his best-selling books are *The Frog in the Kettle, User Friendly Churches, The Power of Vision, Marketing the Church* and *Evangelism That Works.* Among his most recent books is *The Second Coming of the Church,* published by Word, which he considers his most significant book. He is a columnist for *Vital Ministry,* a magazine for church leaders and writes a newsletter distributed by E-mail (available upon request). He is also featured on numerous videotape and audiotape presentations regarding trends, faith, churches and popular culture.

He has served on the faculty of several universities and seminaries. In addition, he has been the teaching pastor at a large, multiethnic church and has been or currently serves on the board of directors of several ministries.

George and his wife, Nancy, were married in 1978. They have two young daughters, Samantha and Corban. The Barna family lives in southern California where they enjoy the beach, movies, music, reading and sports.

Reliable Strategic Information

For nearly two decades, George Barna and his team at Barna Research have been carefully and strategically tracking the relationship between the Church and American culture. Today, Barna Research maintains the most comprehensive database on the spiritual condition of the nation. And they want to help make that information available to you so that your ministry operates as strategically and effectively as possible.

There are various ways of accessing the information Barna Research makes available. Here are some ways of getting the strategic insight you need to minister more effectively.

- *Check the Website*
  Visit www.barna.org for statistics, analysis, resources and more. We offer a free E-mail, sent regularly, to keep you aware of our latest findings.

- *Access Books, Tapes, Videotapes and Reports*
  Barna Research has more than three dozen published resources available for your use. To discover what is currently available, call or write for a catalogue, or explore the company's website (www.barna.org).

- *Attend Seminars*
  Every two years Barna Research Group provides a new seminar for church leaders. These day-long seminars provide insight into the latest research findings and their implications for ministries. Contact BRG for information by phone, mail or website regarding the current seminar and schedule.

- *Commission Custom Research*
  Every year the Barna Research Group conducts studies for dozens of ministries. Those studies are designed to answer the pressing questions and explore potential opportunities facing ministries, from churches to parachurch ministries. Contact the company to discuss the possibilities of engaging BRG to discuss the potential for developing a study that will address your unique needs and opportunities.

Contact

Barna Research
Barna Research Group, Ltd.
5528 Everglades Street · Ventura, CA 93003

(Mon-Fri, 9-5:30, Pacific time)
Voice: 805-658-8885
Orders only: 1-800-55-BARNA
Fax: 805-658-7298
Website: www.barna.org